The Rule of Benedict

The Rule of Benedict

The Saint Meinrad Translation with an Introduction

BENEDICT OF NURSIA

Translated By
Harry Hagan, OSB
Hillary De Jean, OSB

Contributors
Kurt Stasiak, OSB
Harry Hagan, OSB

SAINT MEINRAD ARCHABBEY
SAINT MEINRAD, IN 47577

Contents

Table of Contents

Foreword

St. Benedict wrote his *Rule for Monks* in the sixth century. Little could he have imagined that his Latin text would not only be translated into practically every language, but also that his guidance would remain the foundational text for monastic life and practice some 1,500 years later.

The *Rule* is essential to a monastic community's – and an individual monastic's – understanding of their vocation. The *Rule* offers not only a general philosophy of the cenobitic life, but also many of the specific ways and means Benedict considered essential for a community of monastics – a group always composed of different ages, backgrounds, temperaments, and talents – to live, pray, and work together in harmony.

Hence readers of the *Rule* – and more importantly, its practitioners – will find not only directives on humility, obedience, and silence, but also on the specific psalms to be said in choir, the qualities and attitudes of monastic officials, and safeguards for claustral peace and fraternal respect.

Studied especially in the first years of monastic formation, each chapter of the *Rule* is also read in most monasteries three times a year so that, as Benedict writes in his 66th chapter, "none of the brothers may make the excuse of ignorance." Indeed, monastics celebrating a golden jubilee or beyond will have heard the *Rule* read publicly approaching some 200 times.

The *Rule* certainly urges monastics on to high ideals, but part of the genius of Benedict is that it also reflects a keen sense of human limitations. An example of the former we find in Chapter 4, in which Benedict specifies 73 "Tools of Good Works," instruments that should be found and used daily in the monastic workshop.

We come across a delightful example of the latter in Chapter 40 as Benedict both expresses the ideal but also acknowledges the reality, writing that "although we read that wine is altogether not for monks, it is, however, impossible in our times to persuade monks of this. So let us at least agree to this: we should not drink to excess but more sparingly."

Not only has the *Rule*, as noted, been translated into virtually every language, but many individual translations in each of those languages have been catalogued. Indeed, probably not too many years pass without another scholar, commentator, or linguist attempting in different words and phrasings to express the latest finds in monastic research. This is most appropriate since there are many who consult the *Rule* as the primary guide or as a supplement to their vocation as monastics, oblates, clergy, and "ordinary" lay men and women.

The longest chapter in the *Rule* is Chapter 7, in which Benedict lays out the "seven degrees of humility." He would indeed have been humbled – no doubt also pleased – to have known of his influence upon so many communities and individuals over so many centuries.

Rt. Rev. Kurt Stasiak, OSB
Archabbot, Saint Meinrad Archabbey

Introduction to the Rule of Benedict (RB)

Table of Contents

St. Benedict of Nursia creates his *Rule for Monks* around 530. Though some have seen him as the founder of western monasticism, the reality is more complicated. Benedict comes after more than two centuries of monastic development, and he sifts through the tradition to create what he calls "this smallest Rule written down for beginners." Some 25 monastic rules appear in the late Roman

Empire, and the RB does not become the standard for all monastic communities until the Synod of Aachen (816-819).

A.   The Development of Monasticism Before Benedict

The monastic movement emerges just before 313 when Constantine makes Christianity a legitimate religion in 313. Already in 270, St. Anthony the Great (251-356) has gone out alone into the Egyptian desert to wage single combat with the devil. The word "monk" comes from the Greek *monos*, meaning "only one" or "alone." More specifically, Anthony also becomes a hermit or anchorite—words that come from the Greek meaning "desert" and "withdraw," respectively. Anthony lives to be 105 years old, and St. Athanasius writes a biography that celebrates his great asceticism and victory over the demonic forces. It makes Anthony the great icon of eremitical monasticism.

With martyrdom no longer a possibility as the heroic expression of the Christian life, many men and women go to the desert to become hermits. They settle around recognized *abbas* and *ammas* (fathers and mothers) who serve as spiritual guides. These hermits hand on their insights in short sayings that later generations collected and organized into *The Sayings of the Fathers [and Mothers] of the Desert.*

St. Pachomius also goes to the desert, but rather than remaining alone, he gathers his followers into communities to live a "common life," which translates the Greek *kenos* (common) *bios* (life: biography, biology). As a result, they are known as cenobites who live in a coenobium. While hermits can establish their own way of doing things, those living a common life must have some guidelines about when and how to pray and eat, work and sleep, as well as other common issues that arise with living together. So, Pachomius writes the first monastic rule for his community. Hundreds of people come, and the women gather around Pachomius' sister, Mary, in their own monastery. At his death in 348, Pachomius has organized these cenobites into associations of monasteries, called the "Koinonia" ("Community").

St. Basil the Great, from a family of saints, writes the classic monastic documents for the eastern Church: the *Small Ascetikon* and the *Great Ascetikon*, also called the *Shorter Rules* and the *Longer Rules*. These rules contain a list of questions to which Basil gives shorter or longer answers. Rufinus translates the *Small Ascetikon* into Latin, which has an important impact on the West and on Benedict.

The first question asks about God's commandments, and Basil answers with the great commandment to love God and our neighbor as ourselves, which becomes his central theme. Very quickly, Basil shows his preference for cenobitic monasticism. To Question 3, he outlines the advantages of living with others: 1) our dependence on others for the basic needs of life, 2) our need for others to point out our faults, 3) our need to belong to a community as the Body of Christ, 4) our need for others who possess different gifts, especially those from the Holy Spirit. As Basil sees it, the hermit's isolation from others makes the practice of charity difficult, if not impossible. The hermits would argue that hospitality serves as their charity toward others. For Basil, charity is the center of the Christian life, which he does not distinguish from the monastic life.

Several monastic rules, for both men and women, are attributed to St. Augustine (354-430), who lived a monastic life before becoming bishop of Hippo. As bishop, he gathers his clergy into a community and composes for them a very short rule that scholars identify with the *Praeceptum*, which is easily found online. Like Basil, Augustine emphasizes charity and the common good, to which he added an emphasis on common ownership with its corollary, the equality of the members. Both Basil and Augustine, with their emphasis on community, have an important impact on Benedict and his *Rule*.

John Cassian (360-435) brings the eremitical tradition from Egypt to France. His *Institutes* describe his vision of monasticism. In the *Conferences*, Cassian provides 24 talks, which, he says, he and his friend Germanus hear from the great abbas of the time. Abba Moses gives the first two—the first on the monastic life and the second on discretion. In Conferences Nine and Ten, Abba Isaac speaks about prayer with a particular emphasis on repetitive prayer: the practice of repeating a word or phrase to focus on God. Like his teacher, Evagrius, Cassian sought union with God, which comes with "purity of heart."

B. The Context of Benedict's *Rule* and the *Rule of the Master*

The sack of Rome in 410 marks the triumph of the barbarian invasion and the decline of the Roman empire. Monasteries, notably those of Eugippius and Cassiodorus, provide places of learning amid the disintegration. A number of monastic rules emerge during this time, including the *Rule of the Master*, abbreviated RM. We do not know the name of the author, so scholars have named him "the Master" from the Latin *magister*, meaning "master, teacher."

This rule, the longest and most detailed, sets out a vision focused on getting to heaven. It makes the abbot the micro manager of the community and regards everything with a suspicious and wary eye. Life is a struggle against sin, the flesh, and the power of the devil. The Master emphasizes obedience, silence, and humility as ways of fighting "self-will," which reflects resistance to the will of God, revealed by the abbot.

Until recently, scholars thought that RM was a later version of the RB, but in 1937, a French monk proposed that Benedict took much of his *Rule* from the *Rule of the Master*. This was monastic heresy for many who saw Benedict as a great original genius. However, the careful scholarship of Adalbert de Vogüé and others (mostly

Benedictines) has proved that Benedict, in fact, relied on the Master's *Rule*, especially in the earlier parts of his rule.

As a result, we can compare the two and see how Benedict cuts, changes, or adds to the Master's *Rule*. However, the Master is not the only influence on Benedict. Coming 200 years after Anthony the Great, he shows the influence of Basil the Great, Augustine, John Cassian, and others. Rather than being an original genius, Benedict proves to be a wise genius who winnows the tradition and finds a middle way.

C. The Organization of the Rule of Benedict

1. *The Prologue*

The Prologue opens with a call for the reader to listen to the Teacher's instruction, and "gladly accept, and carry out in full the counsel of a loving Father" (P 12). After urging the reader to turn this teaching into deeds, Benedict concludes with a line from the Master, calling for the establishment of "a school of the Lord's service." Then, Benedict adds his own words and shows us what is central to his vision:

> [46] As for its method of instruction, we hope to establish nothing harsh or burdensome, [47] but if reason and fairness dictate being a little stricter to correct faults or to preserve love, [48] do not then and there become daunted by fear and run from the way of salvation. There is no beginning except a narrow beginning. [49] But, when you have advanced in *conversatio* and in faith, you will run with your heart enlarged and with the unspeakable sweetness of love on the way of God's commands. (P 46-49)

This addition reveals Benedict's humanity and moderation, which are hallmarks of the RB. Early manuscripts changed the word *conversatio* to *conversio*—conversion, but *conversatio* means "to turn continually" and refers to a way of life. Benedict uses the word in several ways to capture the turning of a person's life day by day into a recognizable monastic witness.

2. *The Kinds of Monks and the Abbot: RB 1-4, 64*

The first seven chapters serve as a theological foundation for the rest of the RB. Benedict draws them largely from the Master, but he continually reshapes the material to make it his own.

The opening chapter discusses the kinds of monks. Though it sets hermits above the others, it also states that no one should retire to a life of solitude unless they have first proved themselves by living the common life. Despite his praise, Benedict does not mention hermits again but focuses on the cenobites who live a common life because they are "the strongest kind" of monks. He mentions two other types: the Sarabaïtes and the gyrovagues. "Whatever [the Sarabaïtes] think and choose, they call holy, and whatever they do not want, they consider unlawful" (1.9). The gyrovagues constantly move from one monastery to another, looking for a free meal.

The *Rule* has two chapters on the abbot. In RB 2, Benedict reworks the Master's chapter to create a caring and attentive superior. The abbot must make no distinction between persons based on their status in society before coming to the monastery. He is to show equal love to all (2.22). He must not overlook faults but should deal with each person individually. Rather than calling on the monk to conform to the abbot, Benedict says that the abbot must "conform and adapt himself to all according to the character and intelligence of each person" (2.32).

In RB 3, Benedict calls on the abbot to seek the counsel of the community in all important matters. The whole community should assemble "because often the Lord reveals to the younger what is better" (3.3). For less important matters, he should consult the seniors.

RB 64, which has no parallel in RM, calls for the election of the abbot by the community or a smaller group "with sounder judgment." Benedict then describes the ideal leader. He grounds this vision in the Greek understanding of virtue as standing in the middle. Generosity means being neither stingy nor close-fisted but somewhere between them. However, the middle is not always halfway but shifts depending on the context. Therefore, Benedict calls discretion, the ability to find the middle, "the mother of virtues" (64.19). Words such as prudence, balance, reason, and consideration appear throughout the *Rule* to undergird this theme.

The chapter also insists that it is more important for the abbot "to be for others than to be over them" (64.8). Therefore, "he should always 'exalt mercy over judgment' so that he himself may find mercy" (64.10; Jas 2:13). In correcting monks, the abbot should "act prudently ... lest in his excessive desire to scrape off the rust, he breaks the pot." The *Rule* also reminds the abbot that he is not above the *Rule* and must answer to God for the responsibility given to him. Commentators see RB 64 as one of the most important chapters in the *Rule*.

Chapter 4 lists 74 good works that monks should work on. Though a few may belong particularly to the monastic life, the list has much to recommend to everyone.

3.   *Obedience, Quiet, and Humility: RB 5, 6, 7*

Chapters 5, 6, and 7 deal with the three virtues important to the Master: obedience, quiet, and humility. The Master demands a submissive, even servile, attitude from his monks. Benedict deletes much of the Master's text and mitigates the remainder in various ways to achieve a better balance. Obedience and humility can be dangerous virtues.

The word "obedience" has its roots in *ob+audire* – "to hear" (audio), and Benedict ties obedience to "listening," which is the opening word of his *Rule*. Everyone who truly listens with ear, eye, and heart knows how to respond. Quiet becomes the context for listening.

The chapter on humility begins with John Cassian's list of the 10 marks of humility (*Institutes*, 4.39). The Master reshapes these marks into a ladder of 12 rungs (RM10): the first rung calls the monk to keep the fear of God ever before his eyes; rungs two to four focus on obedience; rungs five to seven deal with humility proper. The eighth rung makes the *Rule* itself and the example of the older members the standard of life. Rungs nine to eleven call for quiet and no foolishness, and the last rung says that a person of true humility reveals that in every aspect of life. This brings a person to the love that casts out fear (1 John 4:18). Benedict adds that the monk will now live not out of dread but for the love of Christ. Humility should bring a person to perfect love.

Michael Casey, OCSO, makes modern sense of this difficult chapter in his book: *A Guide to Living in the Truth*. Casey argues that humility does not mean being a doormat or putting yourself down. Rather, true humility is the radical acceptance of the truth about myself—both the good and the bad, not just the bad. As such, humility is bound to the cross, the great Christian image of reality. Only by embracing the cross can a person come to resurrection.

4.   *The Liturgical Section: RB 9-20, 52*

The section on the community's prayer follows in RB 9-20. Though the Master deals with this much later in his rule, Benedict has placed it second to underline its importance.

These chapters describe the common prayer of the monastery. The two most important times are morning and evening prayer, called Matins or Lauds and Vespers. During the day, the monks pray briefly at the first, third, sixth, and ninth hours. The community says Compline right before bed, and during the night, they rise for the longest prayer, Vigils. Earlier, monastic communities rose at midnight for Vigils, but Benedict pushes it later so that monks, as he says, can digest their food. In reality, the later hour of 2:30 a.m. gives them time to get the deep sleep they need.

RB 19 and 20 give some basic guidance about prayer. Benedict says that prayer should be made "with all humility and pure devotion" and, following John Cassian, "with purity of heart" "so that our minds may be in harmony with our voices." He calls this communal prayer "the Work of God" (*Opus Dei*), for it is both the work that the community does in service to their Creator and also the work that God performs on the individuals to conform them to Christ. As a result, the church or oratory of the monastery should be reserved for prayer alone (RB 52).

5.   *The Discipline of Those at Fault: RB 23-30, 43-46*

Benedict has had enough experience with people to know that some people can "be stubborn or disobedient or proud or a murmurer"; they may oppose "the Holy Rule" or "despise the instructions of his seniors." Benedict pointedly condemns murmuring because this negative gossiping undermines a community's goodwill (34.6).

As in Matt. 18:15-20, the senior monks should counsel the individual privately a first and second time. If a person does not change, he should "be subject to excommunication if he understands the nature of that punishment" (23:4). For Benedict, the worst punishment comes with excommunication—being cut off from the community. This should bring people to their senses. Benedict recognizes that these faults can be more or less serious and that the superior must care for the person at fault "*lest too much sadness swallow him up*" (2 Cor 2:7; RB 27.3). The abbot may need to send another person secretly to console the person. Still, after everything has been done, Benedict recognizes that, in some sad situations, the abbot must expel a person for the sake of the common good (RB 28).

6. The Goods of the Monastery and the Manager: RB 21-22, 31-42 47-51, 53-57, 65

RB 31 calls for the abbot to appoint a manager for the monastery "who is wise and mature in character, temperate, not forever hungry nor arrogant, not troubled nor hurtful, not late nor wasteful; rather, fearing God, he is to be like a father to the whole community" (31.1-2). In short, he is to be like the abbot. Twice, the chapter insists on the importance of humility for the manager lest he use his position for power rather than service. It also put under his protection those without power: the infirm, the young, the guests, and the poor (31.9). The *Rule* counsels him to regard all the monastery's goods as "the consecrated vessels" of the church. This sentence sanctifies every dimension of life. The chapter reminds the manager several times that he is not the abbot, and RB 65 states the same for the prior. The language suggests that there had been problems in the past.

Benedict was absolutely against private ownership (RB 33). The monk must depend upon the abbot and monastery for everything. This mandate is different than St. Francis' insistence on poverty. Benedict's insistence falls on communal sharing and the common good. At the same time, the abbot must recognize the individual differences of the monks, their different strengths and weaknesses. Therefore, the abbot should see that each monk should get what he needs.

Benedict recognizes that any group that cannot care for the sick is not a community. Therefore, he begins RB 36: "Before all and above all, they must take care of the sick in order to serve them truly as Christ." Benedict sets aside a place for the sick and also a person to care for them "who is God-fearing, loving, and caring" (36.7). These innovations underline Benedict's care for the individual.

Simplicity and moderation should characterize food, drink, and clothing. The monastic day divides into the *Opus Dei* – the Work of God (meaning the communal prayer in the oratory), *lectio divina* – divine reading (the slow reading of Scripture that forms the basis for private prayer), and manual labor. The balance among these shifts with the seasons. The summer requires more manual labor, and Lent receives more *lectio divina* than other times (RB 48).

In RB 49, Benedict says that "the life of a monk ought to have at all times the mark of Lenten observance," but he recognizes that most do not have the strength for this. The purpose of Lent, however, is not just asceticism; rather, these Lenten practices should bring a person to "the joy of spiritual longing," which "with the joy of the Holy Spirit," should lead a person to the celebration of Easter.

Benedict calls the monks to treat three groups as Christ because each can cause problems: the abbot, the sick, and the guests. The abbot, who takes the place of Christ, can ask a monk to do something he doesn't want to do. The sick are sick all day long and every day, and Benedict makes the service to them the service to Christ. Finally, guests come at all hours with various needs. The Master in his *Rule* is wary of guests, but Benedict shows none of this wariness to outsiders. Instead, he receives them as Christ "with all humanity" (53.9). So, when guests arrive at the gate of the monastery, the porter cries out "Thanks be to God!" or "Bless me!" because they come as Christ himself (66.3).

Finally, those who pursue a craft in the monastery should carry out their work with humility for the good of the monastery and not for their own self-importance (RB 57). The common good must take precedence.

7.   *The Reception of New Members, Priests, and Other Monks: RB 58-63*

RB 58 says the community should test those wanting to join to see whether they are persistent. If so, they should be given a place first in the guest house and then in the novitiate. The abbot should put them under the charge of "one skilled in gaining souls who should watch over them assiduously in everything" (58.6). The novice master must try to learn "whether he truly seeks God," a phrase often taken as the short definition of the monastic life. Benedict then gives the following criteria for this judgment: "whether he is serious about the Work of God, obedience, and criticism." The "Work of God" refers to the community's prayer, obedience at this stage requires giving oneself to the life of the particular community, and criticism touches humility and living in the truth of oneself. "They should be told everything hard and difficult whereby one goes to God" (58.7-8).

The period of trial lasts for one year. Today in many monasteries, a yearlong novitiate is followed by three years of temporary commitment before a person makes solemn or perpetual vows. RB 58 calls for the monk to make vows of obedience, stability, and *conversatio.* Obedience is the gift of self to the community. Stability ties the person to a specific monastery. As is often said, a monastic vocation is not a call to a way of life but a call to a specific community and its realization of the tradition. *Conversatio* refers to the monastic way of life, and the vow pledges you to give yourself day by day, more and more, to this way of life. The monk makes his vows before the abbot and saints of the monastery, representing the larger Church already in heaven. After signing the document on the altar, the monk receives the monastic habit that reminds him of what he has vowed.

Unlike the Master, Benedict makes provisions for receiving priests and for ordaining monks for the service of the community. However, the *Rule* insists that they must keep the whole *Rule* and be examples of humility (RB 60, 62). Likewise, if monks from other monasteries want to join, the abbot receives them only if they are worthy and join with the permission of their previous abbot (RB 61).

8.   *The End of the Rule: RB 66-73*

Various commentators believe that RB 66 formed the first ending of the *Rule* with its call for reading the text often in the community.

RB 67 deals with monks traveling outside the monastery—a

concern that appears elsewhere. Benedict's insistence on monks being bound closely to the monastery becomes a problem for St. Francis and St. Dominic, who want to send their members out to preach and minister among the people of God wherever needed. As a result, they establish a new type of community with evangelical vows of poverty, chastity, and obedience.

RB 68 deals with a monk being asked to do something he feels he cannot do. Benedict counsels against pride and defiance, but has the monk present his feelings at a proper time. Sometimes another can see potential that we cannot, so Benedict says that if the superior still believes the task possible, the monk, "confident in the help of God," should "obey out of love." Significantly, love becomes the ground of obedience.

RB 69-71 deal with relationships among members. Living together is not always easy, and tensions can arise. For this reason, Benedict has the Lord's Prayer recited at the end of Lauds and Vespers (13.12-14). RB 71 calls for mutual obedience—the obedience of the members to each other. There are then four calls to obedience in the *Rule*: obedience to God, to the abbot, to the other members, and to oneself—the best part of oneself. By being attentive, the monk can anticipate what is needed.

RB 72 on the good zeal of monks summarizes the whole *Rule*. Five statements focus on the relationship to others. The most famous is perhaps the second: "Let them bear most patiently with one another's weaknesses, whether of body or of character" (72.5). People can only change if we accept and love them as they are; even then, they may not change. Then "in love," they are to "fear God." After this, Benedict calls for the monks to "love their abbot with a sincere and humble love" (72.10). The person in charge is very vulnerable, and Benedict is careful to protect the abbot. Finally, the overriding goal is to "prefer nothing whatever to Christ" so that together He might bring us to everlasting life.

The final chapter of the *Rule* directs those "hurrying toward the perfection of *conversatio*" to read the Scriptures, the classics of monastic life by John Cassian, and Basil the Great. As for the present document, Benedict characterizes it as "this smallest Rule written down for beginners." He does not offer it as a grand model of perfection, but only as a place to begin. Perhaps, because of that, the *Rule of Benedict* has served those inside and outside of monasteries for 1,500 years.

D.   A History of the Rule: Its Text and Translations

Though written around 530, the *Rule of Benedict* for almost 300 years is but one among some 25 monastic rules. People recognize its value and begin to copy it. The oldest extant copy, an English manuscript called Hatton 48, dates from the early eighth century.

Charlemagne, king from 768 to 814, unifies his kingdom around standard documents in law, liturgy, music, etc. He had the monks of Monte Cassino make him a copy of Benedict's autograph and send it to Aachen. Monks from Reichenau make a copy that survives in the great Library of St. Gall as the best copy. The Synod of Aachen (816-819) decrees that the RB will be the only rule for all monastic communities.

While they accept this decision, their living tradition is much broader than what Benedict conceived. Carolingian monasteries have schools that train officials for the empire. Monks also serve the government, society, and the broader Church in various roles. Monasteries integrate the people of their neighborhoods into their work. As a result, monasteries adapt the RB to an already existing and vibrant tradition. Monks attempt to live the *Rule* more literally only with the Cistercian reform in the early 1100s. To do that, the Cistercians create a second group of monks, the lay brothers, who take care of the practicalities while the choir monks give themselves to prayer.

Gregory the Great wrote the only existing life of Benedict in the second book of his *Dialogues*. It includes a meeting between

Benedict and his sister Scholastica, who was part of a monastic community of women. She famously prayed for a thunderstorm to prevent Benedict from returning to his monastery so that they spend a last night in holy conversation. Many women have lived and continue to live the monastic life shaped by this *Rule*. In the Middle Ages, they created feminine versions of the RB for themselves, and their life produced great saints such as St. Hilda, St. Hildegard, and St. Gertrude the Great, among others.

The suppression of monasteries in England and later in northern Europe broke the tradition, but it also brought about new foundations and a rethinking of monastic life and practice. Since Vatican II, Benedictine women, led by Joan Chittister, OSB, and Mary Collins, OSB, among others, have worked to give monastic life a new and broader vitality.

The 20th century also produced important monastic scholars: Adalbert de Vogüé, OSB, Aquinata Böckmann, OSB, Terrence Kardong, OSB, and Michael Casey, OCSO, among others. This translation stands on their modern scholarship.

Other modern translations exist. Those from the 20th century, such as RB 1980, offer the reader an idiomatic translation that speaks to the modern context. Recently, Judith Sutera, OSB, published a gender-neutral translation so that its many readers can hear an inviting voice. Each translation has its own value and audience.

This translation seeks a rather literal rendering of the Latin text that reflects its original cultural context. It preserves some Latin words, particularly *conversatio*. The early scribes replaced *conversatio* with *conversio* (conversion), but modern scholarship has restored the original word, which can mean the monastic way of life or the beginning of monastic life. To help readers recognize this keyword, I have left it untranslated so that readers can make their own judgment. The same is true for *lectio divina* – divine reading. Where possible, the text uses the same word for the Latin so that the reader can recognize the continuity. Benedict was not a great Latin stylist, and the translation reflects that reality. As a literal translation, it recognizes the distance between the world of the text and our world, and it demands that we work to discover a relationship between the two worlds.

The *Rule of Benedict* has been a foundational document for western culture since Benedict and the time of Charlemagne. Today it undergirds communities throughout the whole world. I hope this digital edition will make the RB available for those studying history and community living. Some things in this document belong to the early Middle Ages, but much transcends its time and holds a wisdom that can shape our search for community today.

E.   Recommendations for Reading: Selected Chapters from the Rule

If you want to read just parts of the *Rule*, I recommend the following:

1. Begin with the Prologue and pay special attention to the opening.
2. RB 72 is the *Rule* within the *Rule*. It deserves careful attention.
3. RB 64 on the abbot lays out Benedict's idea of an ideal human being. RB 2 contributes to this vision, and RB 3 balances the abbot's authority with the community's counsel.
4. RB 4 lists 74 "tools of good works" that a monk should use; however, most of them are not particularly monastic but apply to Christians and to people in general.
5. An initial reading of the chapters on obedience, quiet, and humility (RB 5-7) can easily misunderstand these virtues; however, 7.67-70 makes clear that the goal of humility is perfect love that casts out fear.
6. In RB 19-20, Benedict gives a very brief introduction to prayer. There he points the reader toward the tradition, especially John Cassian's teaching on prayer and purity of heart in Conferences 9 and 10.

7. RB 58 along with the end of the Prologue (45-50): RB 58 provides a way for integrating new people into a community, and the end of the Prologue offers a succinct statement of monastic life.

8. I call RB 31 on the manager the beautiful chapter because it celebrates humble service for the common good. The following chapters fill this out, especially RB 36 on the sick, which begins: "Before all and above all, they must take care of the sick in order to serve them truly as Christ."

9. RB 53 on the reception of guests fits with the sick because both must be treated as Christ together with the abbot. Benedict's openness to guests reflects his openness to the larger world. He is not isolating himself or his community.

10. RB 73 concludes the *Rule* and claims that this document is only "this smallest Rule written down for beginners" and recommends the Scriptures, the *Conferences* and *Institutes* of John Cassian, and the Rule of Basil the Great "hurrying toward the perfection of *conversatio*."

F.   Short Bibliography

Casey, Michael, OCSO. *Strangers to the City: Reflections on the Beliefs and Values of the Rule of Saint Benedict.* Paraclete Press, 2013.

Chittister, Joan, OSB. *The Rule of Benedict: A Spirituality for the 21st Century.* Crossroads, 2017. This commentary brings the perspective of a Benedictine woman who has served as the prioress of her community.

John Cassian. *Conferences.* Translated by Colm Luibheid. Paulist Press, 1985. A selection from the 24 conferences by the fathers of the desert to John Cassian and his monastic friend Germanus.

Kardong, Terrence G., OSB. *Benedict's Rule: A Translation and Commentary.* The Liturgical Press, 1996. This scholarly commentary explores the relationship of the *Rule* to the tradition.

Stewart, Columba, OSB. *Prayer and Community: The Benedictine Tradition*. Orbis Books, 1998. An introduction to the building blocks of monasticism.

Vogüé, Adalbert de, OSB. *Reading Saint Benedict: Reflections on the Rule*. Translated by Colette Friedlander. Cistercian Studies Series, 151. Kalamazoo, MI: Cistercian Studies, 1994. Fr. Adalbert, one of the great scholars on the *Rule*, comments on the text for novices.

Fr. Harry Hagan, OSB
Feast of Saint Meinrad
21 January 2023

The Prologue

Listen, O my son, to the instructions of the Teacher, and bring near the ear of your heart. Gladly accept, and carry out in full the counsel of a loving Father, [2] so that you may return through the labor of obedience to the one from whom you have backed away through the idleness of disobedience.

[3] To you, therefore, I now direct my words— whoever you may be—to you who renounce your own desires and take up the most powerful and magnificent weapons of obedience in order to fight for the Lord Christ, the true King.

[4] First of all, when beginning any good work, beg him with most urgent prayer to bring it to completion [5] so that he who has already deigned to number us among his children may never be grieved by our evil deeds. [6] For at all times, he should find his good gifts evident in us so that not only may he never, as an angry father, disinherit his children, [7] but even more that he may not, as a dread lord, provoked by our evil deeds, hand us over as most wicked servants to everlasting punishment for refusing to follow him to glory.

[8] Therefore, let us even now rise up since the Scripture rouses us, saying:

> Now is the hour for us to rise from sleep. (Rom 13:11)

[9] And with our eyes open to the deifying light, let us with attentive ears hear what the divine voice counsels us as it cries out daily and says:

> [10] If today you hear his voice,
> harden not your hearts. (Ps 95:8)

[11] And again:

> Whoever has ears to hear,
> let him hear what the Spirit is saying to the Churches. (Rev 2:7)

¹² And what does he say?

> Come, children, and hear me;
> I shall teach you the fear of the Lord. (Ps 34:12)
>   ¹³ Run while you have the light of life
> that the darkness of death may not overtake you. (John 12:35)

¹⁴ And the Lord addresses these things to a great number of people, and, seeking among them his own workman, he says:

> ¹⁵ Who is there that longs for life
> and desires to see good days? (Ps 34:13)

¹⁶ If hearing this, you reply, "I do!" then God says to you,
   ¹⁷ If you want to have true and everlasting life,

> Keep your tongue from evil
> and your lips from speaking deceit.
> Turn from evil, and do good.
> Seek peace, and pursue it. (Ps 34:14-15)

¹⁸ And when you have done these things,

> my eyes will be upon you,
> and my ears will be open to your prayers,
> and before you call on me,
> I shall say to you: 'Look! I am here.' (Ps 34:16; Isa 58:9)

¹⁹ What is sweeter to us, most beloved brothers, than this voice of the Lord inviting us? ²⁰ Behold, in his loving devotion, the Lord shows us the way of life.

²¹ Therefore, having girded ourselves for battle with faith and the keeping of good works, let us, with the Gospel as our guide, go forward on his paths so that we may deserve to see him *"who calls us into his kingdom"* (1 Thes 2:12).

²² If we want to dwell in the tent of his Kingdom, we can never

reach it unless we run there by doing good works. ²³ So let us with the Prophet ask the Lord, saying to him:

> Lord, who shall dwell in your tent,
> or who shall find rest on your holy mountain? (Ps 15:1)

²⁴ After this question, brothers, let us hear the Lord responding and showing us the way to that very tent, ²⁵ and saying:

> The one who walks without fault and does justice;
> ²⁶ who speaks the truth in his heart,
> and has not used his tongue to deceive,
> ²⁷ who has done no evil to his neighbor,
> and has allowed no slander against his neighbor. (Ps 15:2-3)

²⁸ This person, having driven from the horizon of his heart the devil with his wiles, has brought to nothing the begetter of evil and his every enticement. Taking hold of his thoughts while still small, he has dashed them against Christ. ²⁹ Such people, fearing the Lord, do not allow their good observance to make them proud; rather they recognize that what is truly good in themselves is not what they are able do but what is done by God, ³⁰ and so they magnify the Lord working in them, saying with the Prophet:

> Not to us, O Lord, not to us,
> but to your name give the glory. (Ps 115:1)

³¹ Likewise, Paul the Apostle did not claim any credit for his preaching but said:

> By the grace of God, I am what I am. (1 Cor 15:10)

³² And again as he says himself:

> Whoever boasts should boast in the Lord. (2 Cor 10:17)

³³ As a result, the Lord says in the Gospel:

The one who hears these, my words, and acts on them, will be like the wise man who built his house on rock; [34] *and the floods came, and the winds blew and beat against that house, but it did not fall because it had been founded on rock.* (Matt 7:24–25)

[35] Having finished with these words, the Lord waits for us daily to respond to his holy counsel, as we must, by our deeds. [36] Therefore, the days of this life are lengthened as a time of truce for the correction of these evil deeds, [37] according to the saying of the Apostle:

Do you not know that the patience of God is leading you to repentance? (Rom 2:4)

[38] For the loving Lord says:

I do not want the death of the sinner,
but that he should be converted and live. (Ezek 33:11)

[39] Therefore, brothers, now that we have asked the Lord about the one who is to dwell in his tent and have heard the instruction for dwelling there, we shall dwell there – but only if we fulfill the dweller's duties. [40] Therefore, we must get our hearts and bodies ready to fight the battle of holy obedience to his commands. [41] And let us beg God to command that the help of his grace assist us with what is barely possible for us by nature. [42] And if we want to flee the punishment of hell and reach life everlasting, [43] then, while there is still time and we are in this body and are able to fulfill all these things by this life of light, [44] we must run and act in a way that will set us free forever.

[45] Therefore, we must establish a school of the Lord's service. [46] As for its method of instruction, we hope to establish nothing harsh or burdensome, [47] but if reason and fairness dictate being a little stricter to correct faults or to preserve love, [48] do not then and there become daunted by fear and run from the way of salvation. There is no beginning except a narrow beginning. [49] But, when you

have advanced in *conversatio* and in faith, you will run with your heart enlarged and with the unspeakable sweetness of love on the way of God's commands.

[50] And so, never departing from his instruction but persevering in his teaching until death in the monastery, let us by patient endurance share in the sufferings of Christ, so that we may also merit to be partakers of his Kingdom.

1. The Kinds of Monks

It is clear that there are four kinds of monks.

^{2} The first are the cenobites, that is, those who live in a monastery serving under a rule and an abbot.

^{3} The second kind are the anchorites, that is, the hermits. These monks are not in the first fervor of *conversatio* but have been tested at length in the monastery. ^{4} Supported and taught by many, they have long since learned to fight against the devil. ^{5} Well-trained, they go forth from the battle ranks of their brothers to the single-handed combat of the desert. Fearless, even without the mutual support of another, they with the help of God have within themselves the strength to fight bare-handed against the evil ways of flesh and thoughts.

^{6} The third is truly a most detestable kind of monk, the Sarabaïtes. Unlike gold tried in a furnace, they have been tried by no rule and have had no experience to teach them; rather, they are by nature soft as lead. ^{7} By their works, they keep faith with the world, and by their tonsure, they are known to lie to God. ^{8} In twos or threes, or even alone without a shepherd, they shut themselves up in their own sheepfolds, not in the Lord's. For their law, they take what their desires want. ^{9} Whatever they think and choose, they call holy, and whatever they do not want, they consider unlawful.

^{10} The fourth kind of monks, called gyrovagues, spend their whole life staying three or four days as a guest in one monastery and then in another throughout the various provinces. ^{11} Always roaming about with no fixed abode and serving their own passions and gluttonous impulses, they are worse in every way than the Sarabaïtes.

^{12} It is better to keep silent about all of these monks and their most wretched *conversatio*. ^{13} Setting these people aside, let us proceed, with the Lord's help, to set up a structure for the strongest kind, the cenobites.

2. The Qualities Required of the Abbot

An abbot worthy of presiding over a monastery must always remember what he is called and must fill the name of superior with his deeds. [2] For he is believed to act in the place of Christ within the monastery, since he is called by that very name, [3] as the Apostle says:

> You have received a spirit of adoption making you children;
> because of this we cry, 'Abba! Father!' (Rom 8:15)

[4] Therefore, the abbot must neither teach nor ordain nor command anything contrary to the teaching of the Lord, whatever it may be. [5] Rather let his command and teaching be mixed into the minds of the disciples as a leaven of divine justice.

[6] Let the abbot always remember that at the dreadful judgment of God, he will have to give an account both of his teaching and then of the obedience of his disciples.

[7] He should know that the shepherd bears the blame for whatever lack of value the owner may find in his flock.

[8] However, it will be another matter if he has used all the skill of a pastor for a restless and disobedient flock, and has shown all manner of care for their diseased actions.

[9] Their shepherd, once acquitted at the Lord's tribunal, can say to the Lord with the Prophet:

> I have not hidden your justice
> within my heart;
> I have declared your truth
> and your salvation,
> but they have condemned
> and despised me. (Ps 40:11; Isa 1:2; Ezek 20:27)

[10] And finally, the penalty for the flock, heedless of his care, will in the end be overwhelming death itself.

[11] Therefore, when anyone receives the name of abbot, he ought to preside over his disciples with a twofold teaching: [12] that is, he should show all that is good and holy more by his deeds than by his words so that he might set before the able disciples the Lord's commands by words. To the hard of heart, however, and to simpler folk, let him demonstrate the divine commands by his deeds.

[13] Let him point out by his own deeds what should not be done, that is, all those things that run against what he has taught the disciples "lest, while preaching to others, he himself should be found counterfeit" (1 Cor 9:27), [14] and God should say to him, a sinner:

> Why do you declare my just statutes
> and take my covenant in your mouth?
> Indeed, you have hated discipline
> and have cast my words behind you. (Ps 50:16–17)

[15] And also:

> Why do you see the speck in your brother's
> eye and do not see the beam in your own? (Matt 7:3)

[16] Let him make no distinction between persons in the monastery. [17] Let no one be loved more than another unless found better in good deeds or obedience. [18] Let no one well-born be placed before one who comes to the monastery from slavery, unless there is some other reasonable cause.

[19] The abbot may put them in whatever seniority seems good to him or justice may demand; otherwise, let them all stay in their own places [20] because, whether slave or free, we are all one in Christ and bear an equal burden of service under the one Lord "because before God there is no distinction of persons" (Rom 2:11; Gal 3:28; Eph 6:8). [21] Only for one reason are we set apart before him—if we are found humble and better than others in good works.

²² Therefore, let the abbot show equal love to all, and let him maintain the same discipline for all just as they deserve.

²³ For indeed in his teaching, the abbot must always keep that saying of the Apostle where he says:

Reprove, entreat, rebuke. (2 Tim 4:2)

²⁴ This means mixing gentleness with severity as circumstances require.

He should show the rigor of a teacher and the loving affection of a father. ²⁵ In other words, he must reprove sternly the undisciplined and the restless, and he must entreat the obedient and the meek and the patient to make greater progress, but we charge him to rebuke and correct the heedless and the defiant.

²⁶ He should not ignore the sins of offenders, but as soon as they begin to sprout, let him do all that he can to cut them off at the root, remembering the fate of Eli, the priest of Shiloh (1 Sam 2:11-4:18).

²⁷ Those having more honor and understanding he should correct with words of counsel a first and second time, ²⁸ but for the unruly and the stubborn or for the proud and the disobedient, let him restrain them at the very first sign of sin with a beating or other corporal punishment, knowing that it is written:

The fool is not corrected with words. (Prov 29:19)

²⁹ And again,

Strike your son with a rod,
and you will deliver his soul from death. (Prov 23:14)

³⁰ The abbot must always remember what he is and remember what he is said to be, and know that from the one to whom much is given, much will likewise be required.

³¹ Let him consider how difficult and how hard the task he has undertaken—the guiding of souls and the being of service to many with regard to their behavior. He will do this for some by kindness, for others by reproof, for still others by persuasion.

[32] Let him so conform and adapt himself to all according to the character and intelligence of each person so that he not only suffers no loss in the flock committed to him, but he even has cause to rejoice in the increase of a good flock.

[33] Above all, let him not, by ignoring or undervaluing the salvation of the souls committed to him, worry about things passing and earthly and fleeting. [34] Rather he should always bear in mind that he has undertaken the guidance of souls for whom he must also one day render an account. [35] And lest perhaps he should plead lack of means, let him remember that it is written:

> Seek first the Kingdom of God and his justice,
> and all these things will be given to you as well. (Matt 6:33)

[36] And again,

> They lack nothing—those who fear him. (Ps 34:10)

[37] Also, he should know that having undertaken the guidance of souls, he must prepare himself to render an account. [38] No matter how large the number of brothers he has under his care, let him know for certain that on the Day of Judgment he must render an account for each and every soul, and, without doubt, for his own soul as well.

[39] And so, ever fearful of the future reckoning of the shepherd for the sheep entrusted to him, he becomes attentive to his own account even as he heeds the responsibilities for others, [40] and as he helps others to change by his counsel, he brings about in himself a change in his own evil ways.

3. Calling the Brothers for Counsel

Whenever the monastery needs to deal with any important matter, let the abbot assemble the whole community and tell them himself what is involved.

[2] After hearing the brothers' advice, let him think it over alone and then do what he judges more beneficial.

[3] Now we have said that all are to be called for counsel because often the Lord reveals to the younger what is better. [4] Therefore, the brothers should give counsel with all the deference of humility, and they should not presume to defend shamelessly the way that it seems to them. [5] Rather, they should let the matter rest with the decision of the abbot so that all may obey what he has judged more advantageous. [6] Yet, even as it is fitting for the disciple to obey the teacher, so also it is right for him to organize everything with foresight and justice.

[7] In all things, therefore, let them all follow this Rule as their teacher, and let no one easily turn away from it. [8] No one in the monastery should follow the will of his own heart; [9] neither should anyone presume to oppose his abbot brazenly inside or outside the monastery. [10] If someone should presume to do so, let him be subject to the discipline of the Rule. [11] On the other hand, let the abbot himself do all things while fearing God and keeping the Rule and knowing that he must, without doubt, render to God, the most just Judge, an account of all his decisions.

[12] If he needs to deal with matters of less importance for the benefit of the monastery, let him take counsel with the seniors only, [13] as it is written:

> Do everything with counsel,
> and afterward you will not regret it. (Sir 32:19)

4. The Tools of Good Works

First of all, "to love" the Lord "your God with all your heart, with all your soul, and with all your strength."

2 Then, "to love your neighbor as yourself." (Matt 22:37-39; Mark 12:30-31; Luke 10:27; Deut 6:5; Lev 19:18)

3 Then, "not to kill." (Exod 20:13-17; Deut 5:17-21)

4 "Not to commit adultery."

5 "Not to steal."

6 "Not to covet."

7 "Not to bear false witness." (Matt 19:18)

8 "To honor all people." (1 Pet 2:17)

9 "Not to do to another what you do not want done to yourself." (Tob 4:16; Matt 7:12; Luke 6:31)

10 "To deny yourself in order to follow Christ." (Matt 16:24; Luke 9:23)

11 "To chastise the body." (1 Cor 9:27)

12 Not to embrace pleasures.

13 To love fasting.

14 To give new life to the poor.

15 "To clothe the naked."

16 "To visit the sick." (Matt 25:36)

17 To bury the dead.

18 To bring help in time of trouble.

19 To console the sorrowing.

20 To make yourself a foreigner to the ways of the world.

21 To prefer nothing to the love of Christ.

22 Not to carry out your anger.

23 Not to seek an occasion for rage.

24 Not to hold deceit in your heart.

25 Not to give false peace.

26 Not to forsake love.

27 Not to swear lest perhaps you perjure yourself.

28 To bring forth truth from your heart and your mouth.

[29] *"Not to repay evil for evil."* (1 Thes 5:15; 1 Pet 3:9)

[30] Not to do wrong, but also to suffer patiently what has been done.

[31] *"To love your enemies."* (Matt 5:44; Luke 6:27)

[32] Not to return the curses of those who curse you, but rather to bless them all the more.

[33] *"To endure persecution for the sake of justice."* (Matt 5:10)

[34] Not to be proud.

[35] Not to drink to excess. *(Titus 1:7; 1 Tim 3:3)*

[36] Not to eat to excess.

[37] Not to be sleepy.

[38] Not to be lazy. *(Rom 12:11)*

[39] Not to be a murmurer.

[40] Not to be a detractor.

[41] To put your hope in God.

[42] To attribute any good that you see in yourself to God and not to yourself.

[43] Always to recognize the evil that you do, and to reckon it as your own.

[44] To fear the Day of Judgment.

[45] To be terrified of hell.

[46] To desire everlasting life with all spiritual longing.

[47] To keep death daily before your eyes.

[48] To guard at all times the actions of your life.

[49] To know for certain that God sees you in every place.

[50] To dash against Christ your evil thoughts as soon as they come into your heart, and to reveal them to a spiritual senior.

[51] To guard your mouth against evil and devious speech.

[52] Not to love much talking.

[53] Not to speak words that are vain or that give rise to laughter.

[54] Not to love much or explosive laughter.

[55] To listen willingly to holy reading.

[56] To devote yourself frequently to prayer.

[57] To confess the evil deeds of your past to God in prayer daily with tears and sighs.

[58] To change these evil ways in the future.

⁵⁹ *"Not to carry out the desires of the flesh." (Gal 5:16)*

⁶⁰ To hate self-will.

⁶¹ To obey the instructions of the abbot in all things, even though he himself, God forbid, should act otherwise, mindful of the Lord's own teaching: *"Do what they say; but do not do what they do." (Matt 23:3)*

⁶² Not to want to be called holy before you are, but first to be in truth what you would be called.

⁶³ To fulfill the commandments of God daily by your deeds.

⁶⁴ To love chastity.

⁶⁵ To hate no one.

⁶⁶ Not to harbor jealousy.

⁶⁷ Not to act out of envy.

⁶⁸ Not to love conflict.

⁶⁹ To flee arrogance.

⁷⁰ And also to revere the seniors.

⁷¹ To love the juniors.

⁷² To pray for your enemies for the love of Christ.

⁷³ To return in peace to anyone with whom you have quarreled before the sun sets.

⁷⁴ Never to despair of God's mercy.

⁷⁵ Behold, these are the tools of the spiritual craft. ⁷⁶ If we have used them constantly, day and night, and return them on the Day of Judgment, we shall gain from the Lord that reward which he himself has promised:

> ⁷⁷ *Eye has not seen, nor ear heard*
> *what God has prepared for those who love him. (1 Cor 2:9)*

78 The workshop where we diligently work at all these things is surely the cloister of the monastery and stability in the community.

5. Obedience

The first step of humility is obedience without delay. [2] This obedience is characteristic of those who value nothing dearer to themselves than Christ. [3] Whether on account of the holy service which they have professed, or on account of their fear of hell, and the glory of eternal life, [4] as soon as a superior has commanded something, they, as though commanded by God, are unable to let anything delay their doing it.

[5] About these the Lord says:

As soon as the ear heard, he obeyed me. (Ps 18:45)

[6] And again to teachers he says:

Whoever hears you hears me. (Luke 10:16)

[7] Therefore, people like this immediately put aside their own concerns and abandon their self-will. [8] At once dropping what they have in hand, they leave unfinished what they were doing, and with the instant step of obedience, they follow with their deeds the voice of the one who commands. [9] And so, as if at the same moment, the command of the teacher and the completed work of the disciple unfold speedily with the swiftness of the fear of God.

[10] The love of the journey toward eternal life urges them on. [11] Therefore, they seize on the narrow way of which the Lord says:

Narrow is the way that leads to life. (Matt 7:14)

[12] They do not live by their own will, nor obey their own desires and pleasures. Rather, they walk according to the judgment and command of another, and while living the common life, they desire to have an abbot over them. [13] Without doubt, people like these conform themselves to that saying of the Lord where he says:

I have not come to do my will but that of the one who sent me.
(John 6:38)

[14] However, this very obedience will be acceptable to God and pleasing to all others only if they carry out what is commanded with no anxiety, no delay, in no way lukewarm, neither with murmuring nor with a show of unwillingness [15] because obedience offered to superiors is presented to God, for he himself has said:

Whoever hears you hears me. (Luke 10:16)

[16] And the disciple ought to offer this obedience with good spirit because "*God loves a cheerful giver*" (2 Cor 9:7).

[17] For, if the disciple obeys with ill will and murmurs not only with his mouth but also in his heart, [18] even though he fulfills the command, still it will not be accepted by God, who sees his murmuring heart. [19] For such a deed, he receives no reward. Rather, he incurs the punishment of murmurers, unless he makes satisfaction and changes.

6. Quiet

Let us do what the Prophet says:

> I said, 'I shall guard my ways
> so that I may not offend with my tongue.
> I have set a guard over my mouth.
> I said nothing and humbled myself,
> and I kept silence from good things.' (Ps 39:2–3)

[2] Here the Prophet shows that if at times we ought to be quiet for the sake of quiet itself, even from speaking good, how much more should we hold back from evil words on account of the punishment of sin. [3] Therefore, even though the words are good and holy and instructive, let permission to speak be given rarely even to the perfect disciples because of the importance of quiet, [4] for it is written:

> In the midst of much talk,
> you will not escape from sin, (Prov 10:19)

[5] and elsewhere:

> Death and life are in the hands of the tongue. (Prov 18:21)

[6] For it is the teacher's place to speak and teach; to be quiet and to listen belong to the disciple.

[7] Therefore, if you must ask the superior for anything, ask with all humility and with the submission of reverence.

[8] However, we condemn and bar forever and in every place offensive humor and idle talk and the stirring up of laughter, and we do not permit a disciple to open his mouth for such talk.

7. Humility

The Divine Scripture cries out to us, brothers, saying,

> *Everyone who exalts himself will be humbled,*
> *and whoever humbles himself will be exalted. (Luke 14:11; 18:14)*

[2] In saying these things, therefore, it shows us that all exaltation is a kind of pride. [3] The Prophet shows us that he has taken heed by saying:

> *O Lord, my heart is not exalted,*
> *nor are my eyes lifted up.*
> *I have not gone after great things*
> *nor wonders beyond me. (Ps 131:1)*

[4] And why?

> *If I was not humble-minded,*
> *if I have lifted up my soul,*
> *will you not also repay my soul*
> *as does a mother her weaned child? (Vulgate Ps 131:2)*

[5] Therefore, brothers, if we want to reach the summit of humility on high and speedily arrive at that heavenly exaltation to which we can ascend only through the humility of this present life, [6] we must, by our ascending actions, raise that ladder which appeared to Jacob in a dream and "*showed him angels ascending and descending*" (Gen 28:12).
[7] Without doubt, we are to understand this descent and ascent as nothing other than this: We descend by exaltation, and by humility we ascend. [8] The raised ladder is itself then our life in this world which, once our heart has been humbled, the Lord raises up to heaven. [9] We declare the sides of this ladder to be our body and soul;

into these sides the divine call has inserted various rungs of humility and discipline for the ascent.

[10] The first step of humility, then, is that a monk, while always keeping *"before his eyes the fear of God"* (Ps 36:2), should flee forgetfulness in everything, [11] and he should be ever mindful of all that God has taught, so that he always turns over in his heart both how hell, because of sin, burns up those who despise God, and how eternal life has been prepared for those who fear God.

[12] Guarding himself at all times from sins and evil ways, whether from thought, tongue, hands, feet, or from self-will and the desires of the flesh, [13] let him consider that he is always and at all times being watched by God, and that God's gaze sees his deeds in every place, which the angels report at all times.

[14] The Prophet points this out to us when he shows just how our thoughts are always present to God, saying:

> *You search the minds and hearts, O God.* (Ps 7:10)

[15] And also:

> *The Lord knows the thoughts of all humanity.* (Ps 94:11)

[16] And he also says:

> *You have understood my thoughts from afar.* (Ps 139:3)

[17] And,

> *Human thought will confess you.* (Vulgate Ps 75:11)

[18] Therefore, so that he might take care concerning his own perverse thoughts, let a sensible brother always say in his heart:

> *Then shall I be blameless before him*
> *if I keep myself from my own iniquity.* (Ps 18:24)

[19] Indeed we are forbidden to carry out our self-will when Scripture says to us:

Turn away from your own passions. (Sir 18:30)

²⁰ And so we ask God in prayer that his will be done in us. ²¹ Rightly, therefore, are we taught not to do our own will when we give heed to what Holy Scripture says:

There are ways that people think right but their end plunges into the very depths of hell. (Prov 16:25)

²² At the same time, we should also quake with fear at what is said about the heedless:

They are corrupt and their own passions have made them abominable. (Ps 14:1)

²³ As for the desires of the flesh, then, let us believe that God is always present since the Prophet says to the Lord:

Before you is my every desire. (Ps 38:10)

²⁴ Therefore, we must take heed to avoid evil desire, because death is posted at the entrance of indulgence. ²⁵ About this Scripture teaches, saying:

Do not go after your lusts. (Sir 18:30)

²⁶ Therefore, if "*the eyes of the Lord look on the good and the bad*" (Prov 15:3), ²⁷ and if the "*Lord always looks down from heaven upon all humanity to see if any understand or seek God*" (Ps 14:2), ²⁸ and if the angels, appointed to watch over us, daily report both day and night to God the deeds that we do, ²⁹ we should take heed at all times, brothers, as the Prophet says in the Psalm, lest God should see us at any time sinking down into evil and becoming useless.

³⁰ Also, he spares us in this present moment because he is loving, and is waiting for us to be changed by this life for the better, so that he does not need to say to us in the future:

These things you have done, and I was quiet. (Ps 50:21)

[31] The second step of humility is that a monk should not love self-will, and should not indulge in fulfilling his desires, [32] but should conform himself by his deeds to the voice of the Lord who says:

> I have not come to do my will, but that of the one who sent me. (John 6:38)

[33] Likewise Scripture says:

> Self-will merits punishment,
> and self-restraint wins a crown. (Passio Anastasiae 17)

[34] The third step of humility is that a person, for the love of God, should place himself under a superior in all obedience, conforming himself to the Lord, of whom the Apostle says:

> He became obedient unto death. (Phil 2:8)

[35] The fourth step of humility is that a monk in this obedience should embrace suffering quietly and consciously when things are hard or go against him, or even when unjust things, whatever they may be, are inflicted on him. [36] Also, being steadfast, he should not grow weary or depart, as Scripture says:

> The one who has persevered to the very end will be saved. (Matt 10:22)

[37] And also:

> Let your heart take comfort
> and wait for the Lord. (Ps 27:14)

[38] Showing how the faithful ought to bear all adversity for the sake of the Lord, the Apostle says in the name of those who suffer:

> On account of you, we suffer death all day long; we are regarded as sheep for the slaughter. (Rom 8:36; Ps 44:22)

³⁹ And, confident in the hope of divine reward, they follow, rejoicing and saying:

> But in all these things we triumph because of him who has loved us. (Rom 8:37)

⁴⁰ And also, in another place Scripture says:

> You have tested us, O Lord,
> you have tried us by fire,
> as silver is tried by fire;
> you have led us into a snare
> and laid heavy burdens on our back. (Ps 66:10-11)

⁴¹ And to show that we ought to be under a superior, it goes on to say:

> You have set people over our heads. (Ps 66:12)

⁴² However, through patience they fulfill the Lord's teaching in hardships and in unjust treatment:

> When struck on one cheek, they offer the other; when stripped of their mantle, they give up their tunic; when drafted to go one mile, they go two. (Matt 5:39-41)

⁴³ With Paul the Apostle, they bear with false brothers, and they bear with persecution, and they bless those who curse them (2 Cor 11:26; 1 Cor 4:12).

⁴⁴ The fifth step of humility is that a monk should not conceal from his abbot, but should confess humbly, all the evil thoughts coming into his heart and the evil deeds committed in secret.

⁴⁵ To this, Scripture urges us, saying:

> Make known your way to the Lord
> and hope in him. (Ps 37:5)

⁴⁶ And again it says:

> Confess to the Lord, for he is good,
> for his mercy is forever. (Ps 106:1; Ps 118:1)

[47] And again the Prophet says:

> I have made known to you my sin,
> and my unjust deeds I have not hidden.
> [48] I said, 'Against myself I shall confess
> my unjust deeds to the Lord,
> and you have forgiven the ungodliness
> of my heart.' (Ps 32:5)

[49] The sixth step of humility is that a monk should be content with all that is worthless and least, and in everything laid upon him, he should judge himself a bad and unworthy workman, [50] saying about himself with the Prophet,

> I have been brought to nothing,
> and I did not know it.
> I have become as a beast before you;
> yet I am always with you. (Ps 73:22–23)

[51] The seventh step of humility is that a monk should proclaim himself lower and more worthless than all; he should do this not only with his tongue, but he should also believe it with the inmost feeling of his heart. [52] Humbling himself, he should say with the Prophet:

> I, however, am a worm
> and not a human being,
> the reproach of humanity
> and the outcast of the people. (Ps 22:7)
> [53] I have been lifted up and humbled
> and confounded. (Vulgate Ps 87:16)

[54] And again:

For me it has been good
that you have humbled me
so that I may learn your commandments. (Ps 119:71, 73)

[55] The eighth step of humility is that a monk should do nothing except what together the common rule of the monastery and the example of the older monks encourage.

[56] The ninth step of humility is that a monk should restrain his tongue from speaking and keep quiet, not speaking until questioned, [57] as Scripture shows:

In much talk there is no escaping sin, (Prov 10:19)

[58] and,

A man full of tongue will not endure upon earth. (Ps 140:12)

[59] The tenth step of humility is that a monk should not be moved easily or quickly to laughter, because it is written:

The fool lifts up his voice in laughter. (Sir 21:20)

[60] The eleventh step of humility is that a monk should speak gently and without laughter, humbly and seriously, with a few, reasonable words, and his voice should not be full of noise, [61] as it is written:

The wise man is known by few words. (Sextus, Enchiridion, 145)

[62] The twelfth step of humility is that a monk should always make known his humility to those who see him, not only in his heart but also in his very body, [63] that is, at the Work of God, in the oratory, in the monastery, in the garden, on the road, in the field, or wherever he sits, walks or stands, with his head ever bowed and his gaze fixed on the earth. [64] Considering himself at all times guilty of his sin, he should consider himself as already brought before the fearful judgment, [65] saying to himself in his heart always what the publican said in the Gospel with his eyes fixed on the earth:

*Lord, I am not worthy, I a sinner, to raise my eyes to heaven.
(Luke 18:13)*

[66] And again with the Prophet:

*I am bowed down,
and I am humbled in every way. (Pss 38:7-9; 119:107)*

[67] Therefore, when he has ascended all these steps of humility, the monk will soon arrive *"at that love"* which, *"when perfect, casts out fear"* (1 John 4:18). [68] Through this love, everything which he was keeping before out of dread, he will begin to keep without effort, as though naturally, and from habit. [69] He will do it no longer out of fear of hell, but for the love of Christ, and because of good habit itself and delight in virtue.

[70] Through the Holy Spirit, the Lord will deign to make this manifest in his workman, now cleansed from evil ways and sins.

8. The Divine Office at Night

During the wintertime, that is from the first of November until Easter, the brothers should rise at the eighth hour, as this seems reasonable, [2] so that, having rested till somewhat past midnight, they might rise with everything already digested.

[3] The brothers who still have some of the Psalter or readings to learn should devote themselves to study during the time that remains after Vigils.

[4] Then from Easter till the first of November, let the hour be adjusted so that after a short interval – during which the brothers may leave the oratory as nature demands – Matins, which should take place at the first light, may follow without delay.

9. The Number of Psalms to Be Recited at the Night Office

During the wintertime, as mentioned above, this verse is to be recited three times at the beginning:

> O Lord, you will open my lips,
> and my mouth will announce your praise. (Ps 51:17)

[2] To this should be added Psalm 3 with the doxology. [3] After this, Psalm 95 with an antiphon, or at least, it should be chanted all the way through. [4] Next follows an Ambrosian hymn, then six psalms with antiphons.

[5] After these have been recited along with a verse, let the abbot give a blessing, and when all are seated on the benches, let the brothers, one after another, read three lessons from the book on the lectern, with three responsories sung between them. [6] Two responsories should be recited·without the doxology, but after the third reading, let the one who sings recite the doxology.

[7] As soon as the cantor begins to recite, let all rise from their seats out of honor and reverence for the Holy Trinity.

[8] Books having divine authority should be read at the Night Office: both the Old Testament and the New, and also commentaries on them, made by renowned and orthodox catholic fathers. [9] Then, after these three readings with their responsories, the remaining six psalms follow and should be sung with Alleluia. [10] After them, there follows the reading from the Apostle, recited by heart, then a verse and the petition of the litany, that is, the *Kyrie eleison*.

[11] And so the Night Vigils comes to an end.

10. How the Night Praise Should Be Done in Summertime

From Easter till the first of November, let them keep the complete number of psalms as stated above, [2] with this exception: Since the nights are short, the readings in the book should be kept to a minimum; so instead of those three readings, one reading from the Old Testament should be recited by heart, followed by a short responsory.

[3] They should carry out all the rest as stated above, so that they recite no fewer than twelve psalms at the Night Office, not counting Psalms 3 and 95.

11. How Vigils should Be Done on the Lord's Day

On the Lord's Day, let them rise earlier for Vigils. [2] At these Vigils, they should keep the length as determined and set out above: six psalms and a verse. Then, when all are seated in seniority at their places on the benches, let there be read from the book, as stated above, four readings with their responsories. [3] Only for the fourth responsory should the cantor recite the doxology; as soon as he begins, let them all rise with reverence.

[4] After these readings, another six psalms follow in order, with antiphons as before, and with a verse. [5] After these, another four readings are also to be read with their responsories in the manner as above.

[6] Next, let them recite three canticles from the prophets, which the abbot appoints; these canticles are sung with an alleluia. [7] After the recitation of a verse and a blessing by the abbot, let four other readings from the New Testament be read in the manner as above.

[8] Then, after the fourth responsory, let the abbot begin the hymn: "We Praise You, O God." [9] When they have finished reciting this, let the abbot read a passage from the Gospel while all stand out of respect and fear.

[10] At the end of the reading, let all respond, "Amen." The abbot then follows with the hymn: "To You Be Praise." After the blessing is given, let them begin Matins.

[11] This order for Vigils should be observed on the Lord's Day at all times — both in summer and likewise in winter, [12] unless perhaps, God forbid, the brothers rise too late. Then some of the readings or responsories will have to be shortened. [13] However, they should make every effort that this does not happen; but if it does, then whoever was careless should make proper satisfaction to God in the oratory.

12. How the Celebration of Matins Should Be Done

At Matins on the Lord's Day, let Psalm 67 be recited first straight through without an antiphon. [2] After that, Psalm 51 is recited with an alleluia.

[3] After this, Psalms 118 and 63 are recited, [4] then the Canticle of Blessing and the Psalms of Praise, a reading from the Apocalypse, said by heart, and a responsory, an Ambrosian hymn, a verse, the Gospel Canticle, the litany, and the conclusion.

13. How Matins on Ordinary Days Should Be Done

On ordinary days, the celebration of Matins should be done in this way: [2] Psalm 67 is recited without an antiphon, drawn out a little as on Sunday so that all may assemble for Psalm 51, which is recited with an antiphon.

[3] After this, two more psalms are recited according to custom, that is: [4] on Monday, Psalms 5 and 36; [5] on Tuesday, Psalms 43 and 57; [6] on Wednesday, Psalms 64 and 65; [7] on Thursday, Psalms 88 and 90; [8] on Fridays, Psalms 76 and 92; [9] on Saturdays, Psalm 143 with the canticle from Deuteronomy divided in two parts, with each followed by the doxology. [10] On the other days, one of the canticles from the prophets is recited as sung by the Roman Church.

[11] After these follows the Psalms of Praise, then a reading from the Apostle, recited by heart, a responsory, an Ambrosian hymn, the verse, the Gospel Canticle, the litany, and the conclusion.

[12] Morning and evening prayer should absolutely never take place without the superior reciting the Lord's Prayer at the end for all to hear because of the thorns from conflicts which typically arise. [13] In this way, the community members may cleanse themselves of this kind of fault by the solemn promise made in that prayer when they say:

> Forgive us as also we forgive. (Matt 6:12)

[14] But at the other offices, let the very last part of that prayer be recited so that all may respond:

> But deliver us from evil. (Matt 6:13)

14. The Arrangement for Vigils on the Feasts of Saints

On the feasts of saints and on all solemnities, Vigils should be done just as we have stated for Sunday, [2] except that the recited psalms, antiphons, and readings should be proper to that day, but the arrangement described above should remain the same.

15. The Times for Reciting Alleluia

From the holy feast of Easter until Pentecost, let alleluia be recited without interruption both in the psalms and the responsories. [2] But from Pentecost until the beginning of Lent, it should be recited each night only with the last
six psalms.

[3] However, on every Sunday outside of Lent, let the canticles, Matins, Prime, Terce, Sext, and None be recited with alleluia, but Vespers is recited instead with an antiphon.

[4] The responsories, however, are never recited with alleluia except from Easter to Pentecost.

16. The Arrangement for the Divine Office during the Day

The Prophet says:

> Seven times a day
> I have recited your praise. (Ps 119:164)

[2] We shall fulfill this sacred number of seven if we carry out the duties of our service at Matins, Prime, Terce, Sext, None, Vespers, and Compline.

[3] For it was concerning these hours of the day that the Prophet said:

> Seven times a day
> I have recited your praise. (Ps 119:164)

[4] As for the Night Vigil, that same Prophet said:

> In the middle of the night,
> I would rise to confess you. (Ps 119:62)

[5] Therefore, at these times, let us return praise to our Creator for the judgments of his justice: that is, at Matins, Prime, Terce, Sext, None, Vespers, and Compline; and let us rise in the night to confess him.

17. The Number of Psalms to Be Sung at These Hours

We have already arranged the order of the psalms for the Night Office and for Matins; let us now see about the hours that follow.

[2] At Prime, let them recite three psalms one by one, and not under one doxology. [3] A hymn for this hour comes before they begin the psalms after the verse: "*O God, come to my assistance*" (Ps 70:2). [4] At the end of the three psalms, a single reading is recited by heart with a verse and the *Kyrie eleison*, and the concluding prayers.

[5] Now let the prayer at Terce, Sext, and None be celebrated in the same way: that is, the verse, the hymns proper to the hour, three psalms, a reading and a verse, the *Kyrie eleison*, and the concluding prayers. [6] If the community is larger, let them sing the psalms with antiphons, but if smaller, let them recite them straight through.

[7] However, the liturgy for Vespers should have four psalms with antiphons. [8] After these psalms, a reading is to be recited by heart; then come the responsory, an Ambrosian hymn with a verse, the Gospel Canticle, the litany, and with the Lord's Prayer the concluding prayers.

[9] Compline ends with the recitation by heart of three psalms. These psalms are recited straight through without an antiphon. [10] After these psalms, there follows the hymn proper to the hour, one reading, a verse, the *Kyrie eleison* and the concluding prayers with a blessing.

18. The Order for Reciting the Psalms

First of all, this verse should be said with the doxology:

> O God, come to my assistance;
> O Lord, make haste to help me. (Ps 70:2)

Then comes the hymn for each hour.

[2] At Prime on Sunday, recite four sections of Psalm 119. [3] At the other hours, that is, Terce, Sext, and None, three sections of the above-mentioned Psalm 119 are said.

[4] Then at Prime on Monday let three psalms be recited, that is, Psalms 1, 2, and 3.

[5] And so let three psalms be recited at Prime each day until Sunday, one after another through Psalm 20, with Psalm 9 in the Latin and Psalm 18 divided in two.

[6] In this way, Vigils on Sunday will always begin with Psalm 21.

[7] At Terce, Sext, and None on Monday, the nine remaining sections of Psalm 119 should be recited, three at each hour. [8] With Psalm 119 completed on these two days, that is, on Sunday and Monday, [9] the nine psalms from Psalms 120 to 128 should be sung at Terce, Sext, and None on Tuesday, three at each hour.

[10] These psalms are always repeated at the same hours every day until Sunday, as also the arrangement of the hymns, readings, and verses, which remains the same for all these days. [11] And so Sunday will always begin with Psalm 119.

12 Now for Vespers each day, four psalms should be sung. [13] They should begin with Psalm 110 and go to Psalm 147, [14] except for those set apart for other hours, that is, Psalms 118 through 128 and Psalms 134 and 143. [15] All the rest should be recited at Vespers. [16] Since there are three psalms too few, those described above that are longer

should be divided, that is, Psalms 139, 144, and 145. [17] But Psalm 117, since it is short, may be joined to Psalm 116.

[18] With the order of the psalms for Vespers now arranged, let the rest be carried out, that is, the reading, responsory, hymn, verse, and canticle as we have determined above.

[19] At Compline, repeat the same psalms every day: that is, Psalms 4, 91, and 134.

[20] With the order of the psalms for the day hours now set, let all the remaining psalms be divided equally for the seven night offices of Vigils. [21] In order to have twelve psalms for each night, those that are longer must, of course, be divided in two.

[22] Certainly we would counsel anyone who perhaps finds this distribution of the psalms unsatisfactory to arrange whatever he judges better, [23] provided that he takes care in every case that the entire Psalter of one hundred and fifty psalms is sung each week, and that it always begins anew at the Night Office on Sunday.

[24] For monks show themselves exceedingly lax in the service that they have vowed if, during the course of a week, they sing less than the entire Psalter with the usual canticles, [25] since we read that our holy fathers briskly accomplished in a single day what we lukewarm monks hope to achieve only in an entire week.

19. The Instruction for Singing Psalms

We believe that the Divine Presence is everywhere and that "in every place the eyes of the Lord watch the good and the evil" (*Prov* 15:3). [2] Most especially, then, we should, without any doubt, believe this when we are present for the Divine Work.

[3] Therefore, let us always remember what the Prophet said:

> *Serve the Lord in fear. (Ps 2:11)*

[4] And again:

> *Sing wisely. (Ps 47:8)*

[5] And:

> *In the sight of the angels*
> *I shall sing to you. (Ps 138:1)*

[6] Therefore, let us consider how we ought to conduct ourselves in the presence of the Divine and his angels. [7] And let us stand to sing so that our minds may be in harmony with our voices.

20. Reverence at Prayer

When we want to bring anything to the notice of the powerful, we do not presume to do so except with humility and reverence; [2] so how much more should we with all humility and pure devotion make our prayer to the Lord, the God of all things?

[3] We should also realize that we are heard not for our many words but for our purity of heart and tears of compunction. [4] Therefore, prayer ought to be short and pure unless perhaps lengthened by the inmost feeling of inspiration from divine grace.

[5] In community, however, let the prayer always be short, and at the superior's signal, let them all rise together.

21. The Deans of the Monastery

If the community is larger, choose brothers of good repute and holy *conversatio*, and appoint them as deans. [2] Let them show care for their deaneries in everything according to the commandments of God and the teachings of their abbot.

[3] Let such people be chosen as deans with whom the abbot may safely share his burden. [4] And they should not be chosen according to seniority, but according to the merit of their lives and their learning and their wisdom.

[5] If perhaps any of these deans is found blameworthy, having become swollen with pride, let him be corrected once, and again, and a third time, but if he is unwilling to change, remove him, [6] and put in his place another who is worthy.

[7] We also require the same for the prior.

22. The Sleeping Arrangement for the Monks

Let each one sleep in a separate bed. [2] They should receive bedding suitable to their way of *conversatio*, as the abbot arranges.

[3] If possible, all should sleep in one place, but if, however, the number does not permit this, let them sleep in tens or twenties with seniors in charge of their care. [4] A lamp should burn continually in the same room until morning.

[5] Let them sleep clothed with belts or cords around them, but they should not have their knives at their sides while they sleep lest perhaps they wound themselves in their sleep. [6] As a result, the monks will always be ready, when the signal is given, to rise without delay and make haste to reach the Work of God before the others, but still with all gravity and moderation.

[7] The younger brothers should not have beds next to each other, but should be mixed with the seniors. [8] Then, as they rise for the Work of God, let them gently encourage one another because the sleepy make excuses.

23. Excommunication for Faults

If any brother is found to be stubborn or disobedient or proud or a murmurer, or to be opposed in any way to the Holy Rule, and to despise the instructions of his seniors, [2] then, according to our Lord's teaching, let his seniors counsel him privately a first and second time (*Matt 18:15-16*).

[3] If he does not change, let him be rebuked publicly before all.

[4] But if, even then, he does not correct this, let him be subject to excommunication if he understands the nature of that punishment. [5] Should he, however, prove unruly, let him be subject to corporal punishment.

24. The Requirements for Each Type of Excommunication

The degree of the excommunication or discipline should fit the type of fault, [2] and the abbot is to weigh and judge the type of faults.

[3] If, for instance, any brother is found guilty of lighter faults, let him be barred from the common table. [4] Now this will be the standard practice for anyone barred from the common table: he will not lead a psalm or an antiphon in the oratory, nor recite a reading by heart until he has made satisfaction.

[5] Additionally, he should receive the food for his meal after the brothers' meal, [6] so that if, for example, the brothers eat at the sixth hour, that brother will eat at the ninth, and if they eat at the ninth, then he in the evening, [7] until by fitting satisfaction he obtains pardon.

25. More Serious Faults

However, a brother found guilty of a more serious fault is to be banned both from the table and also from the oratory. [2] None of the brothers is to join him for any fellowship or conversation. [3] Let him work alone at his assigned task and endure the sorrow of repentance while remembering that dreadful sentence of the Apostle, who said:

> [4] One like that is handed over for the destruction of the flesh so that the spirit may be saved on the Day of the Lord. (1 Cor 5:5)

[5] He should take the food for his meal alone, both in the measure and at the time that the abbot thinks best for him. [6] No one passing by should bless either him or the food given to him.

26. Those Associating with the Excommunicated Without a Command

If any brother presumes, without the abbot's command, to associate in any way with the excommunicated brother, or to speak with him or to send him a message, [2] let him be given a similar punishment of excommunication

27. The Abbot's Care for the Excommunicated

The abbot should show every care and concern for the offending brothers, for "*it is not the healthy who need a physician, but the sick*" (Matt 9:12). [2] And therefore, like a wise physician, he should use every possible means and send *senpectae*, that is, wise senior brothers. [3] They should console the agitated brother secretly, as it were, and call on him to make the satisfaction born of humility. Also, they should "*console him lest too much sadness swallow him up*" (2 Cor 2:7). [4] Moreover, as the Apostle also says,

> Assure him of your love. (2 Cor 2:8)

And let all pray for him.

[5] For the abbot must show outstanding care, and must move quickly with all shrewdness and diligence, lest he lose any of the sheep entrusted to him. [6] He should know that he has received the care of souls that are weak, and not a high-handed rule over the healthy.

[7] And let him fear the prophet's warning by which God said:

> You would claim for yourself what you saw as fat, and what was weak you would throw out. (Ezek 34:3–4)

[8] Let him imitate the loving example of the Good Shepherd, who left the ninety-nine sheep on the mountains and went to seek the one that had gone astray. [9] He had such compassion for its weakness that he deigned to lay it on his own sacred shoulders, and so carry it back to the flock (*Luke* 15:5).

28. Those, Though Often Corrected, Who Are Unwilling to Change

If any brother has been frequently corrected for some fault and even excommunicated, but still has not changed, let a more stinging punishment come to bear on him: that is, proceed to punish him with the rod.

[2] If, even then, he does not correct it, or perhaps, God forbid, carried away with pride, he even wants to defend his deeds, then let the abbot act as a wise physician. [3] If he has applied compresses, if also the oil of encouragement, if the medicine of the Holy Scriptures, and if at last the cauterizing fire of excommunication or strokes of the rod, [4] and if even then he sees that his diligence achieves nothing, let him then make use of something greater: prayer for the brother, both his own and that of all the brothers, [5] so that the Lord, who can do all things, may work a cure for the sick brother.

[6] If even in this way he is not healed, let the abbot only then use the instrument for amputation, as the Apostle says:

Remove the evil one from your midst. (1 Cor 5:13)

[7] And again:

If the unbeliever departs, let him depart. (1 Cor 7:15)

[8] In this way, one sick sheep will not infect the whole flock.

29. Receiving Back Brothers Who Have Left the Monastery

If a brother who has left the monastery through his own fault wants to return, let him first promise to change everything that caused him to leave, ^{2} and then let him be received back into the last place to test in this way his humility.

^{3} If he goes away a second time, let him be received back, and even a third time, but after that, he should know that every opportunity to return will be denied him.

30. The Correction of Young Boys

Every age and intellectual ability ought to have its proper measure. [2] Therefore, whenever there are boys and adolescents or others less able to understand the gravity of excommunication as a punishment, [3] let such individuals, when they commit an offense, be restrained either by severe fasts or sharp blows so that they may be healed.

31. The Manager of the Monastery

Let there be chosen from the community a manager for the monastery who is wise and mature in character, temperate, not forever hungry nor arrogant, not troubled nor hurtful, not late nor wasteful; [2] rather, fearing God, he is to be like a father to the whole community.

[3] Let him take care of everyone and everything, [4] but do nothing without the abbot's command. [5] Whatever is commanded he should guard.

[6] He should not grieve the brothers. [7] If perhaps some brother asks him for something without a good reason, let him not grieve the person by spurning him, but let him with reason and humility deny the one who has made this improper request.

[8] He should guard his own soul, remembering always that apostolic saying:

> The one who manages well will acquire for himself a good place. (1 Tim 3:13)

[9] For the infirm, the young, the guests, and the poor, he should show every care and concern, knowing and not doubting that he will have to render an account for them all on the day of judgment.

[10] Let him look upon all the vessels and all the goods of the monastery as though they were the consecrated vessels of the altar. [11] Under his leadership, nothing should be neglected. [12] He should not pursue greed; nor should he be wasteful or squander the goods of the monastery; rather, let him do all things with measure and according to the abbot's command.

[13] Above all things, let him have humility, and if he does not have the resources to grant something, let him offer a kind response, [14] as it is written:

A good word is above the best gift. (Sir 18:17)

[15] Everything that the abbot entrusts to him, he should have under his own care, and he should not presume to do whatever the abbot has forbidden him. [16] To the brothers, let him offer without any vainglory or delay their appointed allowance of food lest it cause them to stumble, and let him be mindful of what the Divine Word says about the reward of anyone who *"causes one of the little ones to stumble"* (Matt 18:6).

[17] If the community is larger, let him be given help so that, with their assistance, he may fulfill the office assigned to him with an even temper. [18] At the proper times, let what needs to be handed out be handed out, and let what needs to be asked for be asked for, [19] so that no one may be troubled or grieved in the House of God.

32. The Tools and Property of the Monastery

With regard to the goods of the monastery—its tools, clothing or other things—let the abbot appoint brothers on whose lives and character he can rely. [2] Then, after deciding what will be useful, let him entrust to them the various tools that they are to take care of and bring back. [3] Let the abbot keep a list of these things so that as the brothers follow each other in these assignments, he may know what he hands out and what he gets back.

[4] If anyone treats the things of the monastery with disregard or carelessness, let him be corrected; [5] if he does not change, let him be subject to the discipline of the Rule.

33. Whether Monks Should Have Anything of Their Own

Above all, this vice must be cut from the monastery at its root: [2] namely, no one should presume to give or to receive anything without the abbot's command, [3] and no one should presume to have anything of his own, nothing at all—neither book nor tablet nor pen—indeed nothing at all, [4] since they are not even free to have control either of their bodies or of their own wills.

[5] Rather they should trust that everything necessary will come from the father of the monastery, and anything that the abbot has not given or permitted they are not free to have. [6] "*Let them all have all things in common,*" as it is written, so that "*no one may call anything his own*" or presume to do so (Acts 4:32).

[7] If anyone is caught indulging in this most wicked vice, let him be counseled once and again. [8] If he does not change, let him be subject to correction.

34. Whether All Without Distinction Should Receive What is Necessary

As it is written:

> Distribution was made to each one as there was need. (Acts 4:35)

[2] By this we do not mean to say that there should be favorites, God forbid; however, there should be consideration for weaknesses. [3] When one needs less, let him give thanks to God and not be sad. [4] However, when one needs more, let him be humbled by his weakness and not become self-important because of the mercy shown to him, [5] and so all the members will be at peace.

[6] Before all else, the evil of murmuring should not appear for any reason whatsoever, by any word or by any sign whatsoever. [7] If anyone is found guilty of this, he should be subject to a more severe discipline.

35. The Weekly Kitchen Servers

The brothers should serve each other by turns, and no one should be excused from kitchen duty except for the sick or those engaged in some crucial service, [2] for in this way they gain a greater reward and greater love.

[3] Let the weak, however, have help so that they may do this without sadness. [4] Indeed, all should have help as the number of the community or the situation of the place may require. [5] If the community is larger, let the manager be excused from the kitchen, and anyone else, as we have said, who is engaged in matters of greater service.

[6] Let all the rest serve one another, in turn, with love.

[7] Let the one finishing the week's service on Saturday do the cleaning. [8] They are to wash the towels that the brothers use to wipe their hands and feet. [9] Then, both the one finishing as well as the one beginning are to wash the feet of all. [10] The utensils of his service he should hand back to the manager clean and intact. [11] The manager should then hand them out to the one beginning, and in this way he knows what he hands out and what he gets back.

[12] Now an hour before the meal, the weekly servers should each receive a drink and some bread over and above the appointed portion, [13] so that they may serve their brothers at mealtime without murmuring or hardship. [14] On solemn feast days, however, they should keep the fast until after the concluding prayers.

[15] On Sunday, as soon as Matins are ended, let both those beginning and those ending their week bow down before the knees of all in the oratory, asking prayers for themselves. [16] Let the one finishing his week say this verse:

> Blessed are you, Lord God,
> who have helped me and comforted me. (Dan 3:52; Ps 86:17)

[17] After the one finishing has said this three times and has received a blessing, the one beginning follows and says:

O God, come to my assistance,
O Lord make haste to help me. (Ps 70:2)

[18] This is also repeated three times by all; and having received a blessing, let him begin.

36. The Sick Brothers

Before all and above all, they must take care of the sick in order to serve them truly as Christ, [2] for he himself said:

> I was sick, and you visited me. (Matt 25:36)

[3] Also:

> What you did to one of the least of these you did to me. (Matt 25:40)

[4] On the other hand, the sick themselves must recognize that they are served for the honor of God, and so they should not grieve their brothers who serve them with their unnecessary demands. [5] Still, they must be patiently borne with because such deeds gain a more abundant reward. [6] Therefore, the abbot shall take the greatest care so that they suffer no neglect.

[7] Let a cell be set apart for the sick brothers, and let there be someone to serve them who is God-fearing, loving and caring. [8] Let the sick use baths as often as it is beneficial, but let the healthy, especially the young, have them less often. [9] Also, let the sick who are very weak eat meat in order to recover, but when they are better, they should all abstain from meat according to the usual custom.

[10] Let the abbot take all possible care that the sick are not neglected by the managers and those serving them. Indeed, he is himself responsible for whatever his disciples fail to do.

37. The Old and the Very Young

Although human nature is itself inclined toward mercy for these ages, namely, the old and the very young, still the authority of the Rule should also provide for them. [2] Let their weakness always be taken into account, and let them not be held to any of the Rule's rigor with regard to food. [3] Rather, let them have the consideration of love, and let them come before the regular hours.

38. The Reader of the Week

There must always be reading while the brothers are at table, and the reader should not be just anyone who happens to be there and grabs the book. Rather, let the one who is going to read do so for the whole week, and begin on Sunday.

[2] Beginning after Mass and Communion, he should ask all to pray for him so that God may keep from him a spirit of pride. 3 Let all recite this verse three times in the oratory, with the reader himself beginning it:

> O Lord, you will open my lips,
> and my mouth will announce your praise. (Ps 51:17)

[4] Then, after receiving a blessing, let him begin to read.

[5] There should be complete silence so that no whisper or voice is heard there except that of the reader alone. [6] Therefore, the brothers should serve each other whatever is necessary for eating and drinking in such a way that no one needs to ask for anything. [7] If, however, something is required, they should ask for it with some signal rather than with their voice.

[8] Let no one there presume to ask a question about the reading itself or about anything else "*lest occasion is given [to the Evil One]*" (*Eph 4:27; 1 Tim 5:14*), [9] unless perhaps the superior wants to say something briefly for their edification.

[10] Now because of Holy Communion, the brother who is reading for the week should receive some diluted wine before he begins to read so that it does not become too hard for him to keep the fast. [11] Then afterwards, he should eat with the weekly cooks and servers.

[12] The brothers should not read or sing according to seniority, but only those who edify the hearers.

39. The Measure of Food

We believe it enough for the daily meal, whether at the sixth or ninth hour, that every table should have two cooked dishes because of the limitations of different people. [2] In this way, a person unable to eat from one may perhaps make a meal of the other. [3] Therefore, two cooked foods should be enough for all the brothers, and if there is any fruit or fresh vegetables available, let a third be added as well.

[4] A generous pound of bread should suffice for a day, whether there be one meal or both a midday meal and a supper. [5] If they are going to have supper, let a third part of the pound be kept by the manager and be given to them at supper.

[6] If the work happens to increase, the abbot has the power to decide and add something more, as seems helpful. [7] In this, they should avoid excess, above all else, so that nausea never surprises the monk, [8] for nothing so contradicts every Christian as does excess, [9] as our Lord says:

> See that your hearts are not weighed down by excess. (Luke 21:34)

[10] The same amount should not be allotted to the younger boys, but less than to the older ones, in order to preserve an economy in everything.

[11] All, however, are to abstain entirely from eating the flesh of four-footed animals, except for the sick who are very weak.

40. The Measure of Drink

Each person has a particular gift from God—one in this way, another in that" (1 Cor 7:7).

[2] Therefore, it is with some unease that we undertake to determine the measure of food and drink for others.

[3] However, while making due allowance for the weakness of the sick, we believe that a hemina of wine a day is enough for each person. [4] But those to whom God gives the strength to abstain should know that they will have their own reward.

[5] If either the nature of the place, or the work, or the summer's heat requires more, the superior has the power to decide this while taking care, as always, that no overindulgence or drunkenness creeps in. [6] Although we read that wine is altogether not for monks, it is, however, impossible in our times to persuade monks of this. So let us at least agree to this: we should not drink to excess but more sparingly, [7] for *"wine makes even the wise fall away"* (Sir 19:2).

[8] When, however, the nature of the place makes it impossible to get even the measure mentioned above, but much less or even none at all, let those who live there bless God and not murmur. [9] This above all do we counsel them: there is to be no murmuring among them.

41. The Time When the Brothers Are to Take Their Meals

From Holy Easter until Pentecost, the brothers will eat at midday and take their supper in the evening. [2] Then, from Pentecost and throughout the whole summer, let the monks fast until the ninth hour on Wednesdays and Fridays, unless they have work in the fields or the summer's heat is too much.

[3] On other days, let them take their main meal at midday. [4] If they have work in the field or the summer's heat is too much, the abbot, as he sees fit, may keep the main meal at midday. [5] In general, let him temper and arrange all things in such a way that souls may be saved and that what the brothers do, they may do without justified murmuring.

[6] From the ides of September, that is, the thirteenth day, until the beginning of Lent, let the brothers always take their meal in the middle of the afternoon. [7] During Lent, however, until Easter, let them take their meal in the evening. [8] Yet, this evening meal should be done in such a way that they will not need lamplight while they eat; rather, everything should be finished while there is still daylight. [9] Indeed, at all times, let the hour, whether for supper or for the one meal, be regulated in a such way that everything may be done by daylight.

42. No One Should Speak After Compline

Monks ought to be eager for silence at all times, and especially during the night hours. [2] Therefore, at all times, whether on fast days or days with a midday meal, let this be the norm:

[3] If it is the season for midday meals, then as soon as they rise from supper, let them all sit together as a group, and let one person read *The Conferences* or *The Lives of the Fathers* or indeed anything that may edify the hearers, [4] but not the Heptateuch or the Books of Samuel and Kings, for it will not be beneficial for those of weak understanding to hear those parts of Scripture at that hour; however, they may be read at other times.

[5] If, on the other hand, it is a fast day, then shortly after Vespers has been said, let them assemble for the reading of *The Conferences*, as we have said. [6] Four or five pages are read, or as many as time allows [7] so that all—even those busy with assigned tasks—may gather as one during this period for reading. [8] Then, when all are assembled as one, let them say Compline, and, after they come from Compline, no one will have permission to speak again to anyone about anything.

[9] If anyone is found transgressing this rule of quiet, let him be subject to a serious punishment, [10] unless some need comes up among the guests, or perhaps the abbot would command someone to do something. [11] Even so, this too should be done with all gravity and moderation.

43. Those Who Come Late to the Work of God or to Table

At the hour of the Divine Office, let them all, as soon as they hear the signal, set aside whatever is at hand and run with utmost speed, [2] yet with gravity, lest they spark some foolishness. [3] Therefore, let nothing be preferred to the Work of God.

[4] Should anyone get to the Night Office after the doxology of the ninety-fifth psalm—and for this reason, we want it to be said very deliberately and slowly— let him not stand in his regular place in choir, [5] but let him stand last of all, or in a place which the abbot has set apart for the careless, so that they may be seen by him and by everyone, [6] until, at the end of the Work of God, he does penance publicly to make satisfaction.

[7] We have decided that they ought to stand in the last place or apart for this reason: that, after being seen by all and feeling their own shame, they might change. [8] For, if they remain outside the oratory, there will be the type who either takes himself back to bed and sleeps, or who perhaps sits outside and wiles away the time talking, and so *occasion is given to the Evil One*" (Eph 4:27; 1 Tim 5:14). [9] Rather, let them come inside so that they may not lose everything and may change for the future.

[10] At the day hours, if anyone arrives for the Work of God after the verse and the doxology of the first psalm, which is recited after the verse, let them stand in the last place according to the regulation, which we stated above. [11] They should not presume to join the choir of those chanting until they have made satisfaction, unless perhaps the abbot, by his pardon, gives them permission. [12] Even so, the one at fault is to make satisfaction for this.

[13] Should anyone fail to arrive at table and make it impossible for all to recite the verse at the same time and to pray and then to sit down together at table, [14] and should he arrive late because of

his own carelessness or fault, let him be corrected for this a first and even a second time. [15] If still he does not change, he should not be permitted to share the common table. [16] Moreover, let him eat alone, separated from the fellowship of all, until he has made satisfaction and has changed.

[17] Furthermore, anyone who is not present for the verse said after the meal should undergo the same.

[18] No one should presume to take any food or drink before or after the appointed time. [19] However, if a superior offers anyone anything, and he refuses to accept it but later wants what he had earlier refused, he should not have either this, or anything else at all, until there has been an appropriate change.

44. How Those Excommunicated Are To Make Satisfaction

Those excommunicated for serious faults from the oratory and the table must, at the hour for celebrating the Work of God in the oratory, lie prostrate before the doors of the oratory, saying nothing. [2] He simply lies there stretched out with his face on the ground at the feet of those coming out of the oratory, [3] and he should continue to do this until the abbot judges that he has made satisfaction.

[4] At the abbot's command, let him come and prostrate himself at the feet of the abbot himself and then at the feet of all so that they may pray for him, [5] and then, if the abbot commands it, let him be received back into the choir and to the place in seniority which the abbot has determined.

[6] Even so, he should not presume to begin a psalm or a reading, or anything else in the oratory, unless the abbot again commands him, [7] and at all the hours, as the Work of God is ending, let him cast himself on the ground at the place where he stands, [8] and he should make satisfaction in this way until the abbot again commands that he may now stop this satisfaction.

[9] Those excommunicated only from the table for minor faults are to make satisfaction in the oratory as long as the abbot commands it; [10] they will continue this until he gives a blessing and says: "Enough."

45. Those Who Make Mistakes in the Oratory

If anyone—while reciting a psalm, response, antiphon, or reading—makes a mistake and does not humble himself before all by making satisfaction, let him be subject to a greater punishment, [2] inasmuch as he was unwilling to correct by humility what he committed through carelessness. [3] Children, however, should be given a whipping for a fault such as this.

46. Those Who Commit Any Other Faults

If anyone does something wrong, while working at whatever job, whether in the kitchen, the storeroom, the office, the mill, the garden, or at some other craft, or in any other place, [2] or breaks or loses anything, or oversteps a boundary in whatever way, [3] and does not come at once before the abbot and the community, and of his own accord make satisfaction and confess his fault, [4] and if it is revealed by another, let him be subject to a greater correction.

[5] If, however, the cause of the sin lies hidden in the soul, let him disclose it only to the abbot or to the spiritual seniors, [6] who know how to cure both their own wounds and those of others without exposing them and making them public.

47. Announcing the Hour for the Work of God

It will be the abbot's duty to signal the time for the Work of God, day and night. Either he is to give the signal, or he may assign this duty to a careful brother, so that all things may be carried out at the proper times.

[2] Then, let those designated intone the psalms or antiphons after the abbot in seniority.

[3] On the other hand, let no one presume to sing or read unless he is able to fulfill that office by edifying the hearers. [4] And let it be done with humility, gravity, and trembling—again, by those whom the abbot has designated.

48. The Daily Manual Labor

Idleness is the enemy of the soul. Therefore, the brothers ought to be occupied at fixed times in manual labor, and again at fixed times in *lectio divina*.

[2] And so, we believe that the times for each should be arranged in this way: [3] that is, from Easter to the first of October, they will set out in the morning and work from the first to about the fourth hour at whatever needs to be done.

[4] From the fourth hour until the time when they have Sext, let them be free for *lectio*. [5] Then, after Sext or when they rise from table, let them rest on their beds in all silence, or perhaps if someone wants to read, let him read in such a way that he will not disturb anyone else. [6] Let them have None somewhat earlier, at the middle of the eighth hour; then let them work again at whatever is to be done until Vespers.

[7] If, however, the needs of the place or poverty requires that they themselves be involved in gathering the harvest, let them not be sad, [8] for then they are truly monks if they live by the work of their own hands, as also did our fathers and the apostles. [9] Even so, let all things be done with measure on account of the weak.

[10] From the first of October to the beginning of Lent, they should be free for *lectio* through the end of the second hour. [11] At the second hour, let them have Terce, and until the ninth hour, all should work at the job which has been assigned to them. [12] Then, at the first signal for the hour of None, each one should set aside his work and be ready as soon as the second signal strikes. [13] After the meal, let them be free for their *lectio* or for psalms.

[14] Now during the days of Lent, they should be free for their *lectio* from morning until the end of the third hour; then, until the end of the tenth hour, they should work at what is assigned.

[15] During these days of Lent, let them all receive separate books from the library, which they should read straight through in their

entirety. [16] These books should be handed out at the beginning of Lent.

[17] Moreover, let one or two seniors be appointed to go around the monastery at these times when the brothers are free for *lectio* [18] to see that no brother is found bored—spending this time for himself in idleness or talk instead of being focused on *lectio*, and so he is not only useless to himself but also distracts others. [19] If, God forbid, you discover a person like this, then correct him a first and a second time; [20] if he does not change, let him be subject to the correction of the Rule so that the others may fear. [21] Moreover, no brother should associate with a brother at unspecified times.

[22] On the Lord's Day, all should be free for *lectio*, with the exception of those who are assigned to various duties. [23] If indeed anyone has become so careless and idle that he is unwilling or unable to study or read, let him be assigned some work that he can do so that he is not idle.

[24] As for those brothers who are sick or fragile, let them be assigned some work or craft so that they may be neither idle nor oppressed and driven away by the pressure of the work. [25] The abbot should take their weakness into consideration.

49. The Observance of Lent

Although the life of a monk ought to have at all times the mark of Lenten observance, [2] few have the strength for this. Therefore, we exhort all alike during these days of Lent to guard their lives by all that is pure [3] and to wash away during these holy days the careless acts of other times. [4] This, then, is done worthily if we refrain from every vice, and give ourselves to prayer with tears, to *lectio*, and to compunction of heart, and also to abstinence.

[5] Therefore, during these days, let us for our own sake add something to our ordinary measure of service, such as private prayers or abstinence from food and drink, [6] so that each of us, of our own free will, may offer to God *"with the joy of the Holy Spirit"* (1 Thes 1:6) something over and above our appointed service. [7] That is, let us deprive our body of food, drink, sleep, much talk, and foolishness. Then with the joy of spiritual longing, let us look forward to Holy Easter. [8] Let each one, however, lay before his abbot what he would offer up, and let it be done with the abbot's prayer and approval, [9] for what is done without the permission of the spiritual father will be reckoned as presumption and vainglory, and not as merit. [10] Therefore, all things are to be done with his approval.

50. Brothers Who Work Far From the Church or Who Are on a Journey

When brothers work at a great distance and are unable to meet in the oratory at the appointed time, [2] and the abbot judges that this is so, [3] let them carry out the Work of God where they work, kneeling down and trembling with godly fear.

[4] Likewise, those sent on a journey should not ignore the established hours, but they, as they are able, should carry them out and not become careless about rendering their measure of service.

51. Brothers Who Do Not Travel Far

A brother who is sent off for some reason, and is expected to return to the monastery that day, should not presume to eat outside, even if he is asked by someone repeatedly, [2] unless perhaps his abbot instructs him. [3] If he does otherwise, let him be excommunicated.

52. The Oratory of the Monastery

The oratory ought to be what it is called, and nothing else should be done or kept there. [2] When the Work of God is finished, let all leave in complete silence, and let reverence for God prevail, [3] so that a brother who perhaps wants to pray alone may not be thwarted by another's unruliness.

[4] And also, if someone else at another time, perhaps, wants to pray by himself, let him just go in and pray, not in a loud voice, but with tears and keenness of heart.

[5] Therefore, anyone not doing work like this should not be permitted to stay in the oratory once the Work of God is finished, so that, as has been said, no one has to endure the interference of another.

53. The Reception of Guests

Let all the guests at their arrival be received as Christ, for he himself will one day say: *"I was a guest, and you received me"* (Matt 25:35). [2] So let fitting honor be shown to all, especially to the household of faith and to travelers.

[3] Therefore, when a guest is announced, let him be met by the superior, or by the brothers, with every service required by love. [4] First, let them pray together, and so be joined to each other in peace. [5] The kiss of peace should not be offered before saying a prayer because of the devil's delusions.

[6] In the greeting itself, let every sign of humility be shown to all the guests as they arrive or depart. [7] With the head bowed or with the whole body cast on the ground, let Christ, who is also received, be adored in them.

[8] After the guests have been received, let them be led to prayer, and afterward the superior or the one designated by him should sit with them. [9] Let the Divine Law be read in the presence of the guests for their edification, and after this, let all humanity be shown to them.

[10] The superior may break the fast on account of a guest, unless perhaps it is a principal fast day which cannot be broken. [11] The brothers, however, are to follow the usual practice of fasting.

[12] Let the abbot pour water on the hands of the guests; [13] then, the abbot, as well as the whole community, should wash the feet of all the guests. [14] After the washing is done, let them recite this verse,

> We have received your mercy, O God,
> in the midst of your temple. (Ps 48:10)

[15] Let great care and concern be shown when receiving the poor and travelers, for in them is Christ more especially received, for the very fear of the rich sees to their honor.

[16] Let there be a kitchen just for the abbot and the guests, who

are never lacking in a monastery, so that the guests, coming as they do at unexpected times, may not disturb the brothers. [17] In this kitchen, let there be assigned for a year two brothers who can fulfill this job well. [18] Let them have help when they need it, so that they may serve without murmuring; on the other hand, when they have less work, let them go and work wherever they are ordered. [19] This should be taken into consideration not only for them, but for all with jobs in the monastery, [20] so that when they have need, they get help, and then when they are free, they should obey what they are commanded.

[21] Also, let a brother with a soul possessed by the fear of God have charge of the quarters set aside for the guests, [22] and enough beds should be set up there.

Moreover, let the House of God be managed wisely by the wise.

[23] Unless instructed otherwise, no one should in any way associate or talk with the guests, [24] but if someone meets or sees them, let him greet them humbly, as we have said, and having asked for a blessing, let him continue on his way, saying that he is not permitted to speak with a guest.

54. Whether a Monk Ought to Receive Letters or Anything Else

On no account should a monk be permitted, without the abbot's instruction, to give or receive letters or blessed objects or small gifts, either from his parents or from any other person, or from one another. [2] If anything is sent to him even by his parents, he should not presume to receive the thing without showing it first to the abbot. [3] Even if the abbot commands its acceptance, he still has the power to command who will receive it. [4] In any case, the brother to whom it was sent should not be sad, so that no occasion is given to the devil (Eph 4:27; 1 Tim 5:14).

[5] Whoever presumes otherwise should be subject to the discipline of the Rule.

55. The Clothing and Footwear of the Brothers

The brothers should have clothes according to the condition and climate of the place where they live, [2] for in cold regions they will need more, but less in warmer regions. [3] Consequently, the abbot has the power to determine this.

[4] Nevertheless, we believe that it would be enough for each monk in a temperate climate to have a cuculla and a tunic, [5] a heavy tunic in winter, and in summer one that is light or well worn; [6] he should also have a scapular for work, and to cover the feet, footwraps and footwear.

[7] The monks should not make an issue of the color or quality of these things, but they should be the kind which can be found in the region where they live, or which can be bought rather cheaply.

[8] The abbot, however, should see to the size, so that these clothes are not too short but fit those who wear them.

[9] Those getting new clothes should always return the old ones at once to the vestry for the sake of the poor, [10] for it is enough for a monk to have two tunics and two cucullas for nights and for washing. [11] Anything more than that is superfluous and ought to be taken away. [12] Also, the footwraps, and whatever else is old, should be returned when they receive something new.

[13] Those sent on a journey should get leggings from the vestry, and on their return they should put them back in their place, washed, [14] Also, cucullas and tunics should be somewhat better than what they usually have; those going out on a journey should get them from the vestry and put them back on their return.

[15] Now for bedding, a mat, a light blanket, a wool blanket, and a pillow should be enough. [16] However, the beds ought to be inspected frequently by the abbot so that no private possession may be found there, [17] and if anyone is found to have something that he has not

received from the abbot, let him be subject to an extremely severe discipline. [18] And so that this vice of having one's own things may be cut off at the root, the abbot should provide all that is necessary: [19] that is, cuculla, tunic, footwraps, footwear, belt, knife, pen, needle, handkerchief, and tablets, so that every excuse for necessity may be taken away.

[20] Still, let the abbot always consider that passage in the Acts of the Apostles:

> To each and every one was given just what each one needed.
> (Acts 4:35)

[21] Therefore, the abbot should take into account the weaknesses of those in need, but not the bad will of the envious. [22] At the same time, he should in all his decisions think about the judgment of God.

56. The Abbot's Table

Let there always be guests and travelers at the abbot's table. [2] However, whenever the guests are few, the abbot may invite any of the brothers he wants. [3] Still, one or two seniors should always be left with the brothers for the sake of good order.

57. The Craftsmen of the Monastery

Should there be craftsmen in the monastery, let them work at their crafts with all humility if the abbot gives permission. [2] But if any of them thinks himself superior because of the knowledge of his craft, in that he seems to confer something on the monastery, [3] let such a person be taken out of that craft and not practice it again, unless perhaps, after he has humbled himself, the abbot commands him to resume it.

[4] If anything crafted by these workers is to be sold, let those who handle the transactions see that they do not plot any fraud. [5] Let them always be mindful of Ananias and Sapphira, lest perhaps the death that those two suffered in their bodies [6] should likewise overtake the souls of the craftsmen and all who commit any fraud with the goods of the monastery.

[7] On the other hand, the evil of avarice should not steal into their prices, [8] but always let the price be set a little cheaper than what others outside are able to set, [9] *that in all things God may be glorified*" (1 Pet 4:11).

58. The Instruction for Receiving Brothers

Anyone newly come to *conversatio* should not be allowed to enter easily, [2] but as the Apostle says:

> *Test the spirits to see whether they are from God.* (1 John 4:1)

[3] Therefore, if whoever comes keeps knocking, and if he shows for four or five days that he patiently bears both the ill treatment inflicted upon him and the difficulties of getting in, and if he persists in his petition, [4] let him be allowed to enter and stay in the guest quarters for a few days. [5] Then after that, let him stay in the novitiate where they are to study and eat and sleep.

[6] Also, let a senior be assigned to them—one skilled in gaining souls who should watch over them assiduously in everything. [7] The concern should be whether he truly seeks God—whether he is serious about the Work of God, obedience, and criticism. [8] They should be told everything hard and difficult whereby one goes to God.

[9] After two months have passed, if he promises to persevere in his stability, let this entire Rule be read to him, [10] and it should be said to him: "Behold the Law under which you want to serve and fight; if you are able to keep it, enter; if, in fact, you cannot, then, you are free to depart."

[11] If he remains steadfast, then let him be taken back to the novitiate, mentioned above, where his patient endurance in everything is again to be tested.

[12] Then after six months have passed, let the Rule be read to him so that he may know what he is entering. [13] And if he remains steadfast, let this same Rule be read to him again after four months.

[14] If then, after his own deliberation, he is ready to promise that he will guard everything and keep all that is commanded him, then let

him be received into the community, [15] but let him also realize what has been established by the law of the Rule: From that day forward it is not lawful for him to leave the monastery, [16] nor may he shake from his neck the yoke of the Rule which after such a prolonged deliberation he was free either to refuse or to accept.

[17] Now then, when he is to be received, let him promise in the oratory in the presence of all his stability and the *conversatio* of his ways and obedience; [18] let him do this in the presence of God and his saints, so he may know that if ever he acts otherwise, he will be condemned by the one whom he mocks. [19] With regard to his promise, let him make the profession in the name of the saints whose relics are in that place and in the name of the abbot who is present.

20 Let him write the profession in his own hand, or at least, if he does not know how to write, let another whom he has asked write it out. Even so, the novice himself should make his mark and with his own hand put it upon the altar.

[21] After placing it there, let the novice himself immediately begin this verse:

> Uphold me, O Lord,
> according to your promise,
> and I shall live;
> and do not confound me
> in my expectation. (Ps 119:116)

[22] Let the whole community respond with this verse three times, adding the doxology. [23] After this, let the newly professed brother prostrate himself at the feet of each person so that they may pray for him, and from that day on, let him be counted as one of the community.

[24] If he has any property, let him first bequeath it to the poor, or let him make a formal gift and bestow it on the monastery, keeping back nothing at all for himself [25] since he knows that he will not even have power over his own body from that day forward.

[26] Then and there in the oratory, he should be stripped of the

clothes that belong to him and be clothed with those of the monastery. [27] Now the clothes that he has taken off should be placed in the vestry and kept there, [28] so that if he should ever consent to the devil's urging to leave the monastery, God forbid, then he may be cast out, stripped of what belongs to the monastery.

[29] Even so, he should not get back his profession which the abbot took from the altar; rather it should be kept in the monastery.

59. The Offering of the Sons of Nobles or of the Poor

If perhaps one of the nobles would offer his son to God in the monastery, and the boy himself is too young, his parents should make the profession which we have spoken about above. [2] Then, together with the offering, let them wrap the profession and the hand of the boy in the altar cloth, and so offer him.

[3] Now as for their property, they must promise under oath in the same profession that they will never, either themselves or through an agent, or in any way whatsoever, give him anything or offer him an opportunity to have anything. [4] Or else, if they are unwilling to do this and want to offer something as alms to the monastery for their own merit, [5] let them make a donation of the property that they want to give to the monastery, keeping for themselves, if they so wish, the income.

[6] In this way, then, each and every way is to be blocked so that no notion may remain for the boy whereby, beguiled, he may perish, God forbid. This we have learned from experience!

[7] The poor should also act in like manner. [8] Those who have nothing at all simply make the profession and offer their son with the oblation before witnesses.

60. Priests Who Perhaps May Want to Live in the Monastery

If someone from the order of priests asks to be received into the monastery, consent should definitely not be given to him too quickly. [2] Yet, if he remains absolutely steadfast in this request, let him realize that he will have to keep the whole discipline of the Rule [3] and that nothing will be relaxed for him, so that it may be as it is written:

> Friend, what have you come for? (Matt 26:50)

[4] Still, he should be allowed to stand after the abbot and to bless or to preside at the Mass, but only if the abbot commands him. [5] Otherwise, he should not presume to do anything whatsoever, realizing that he is subject to the discipline of the Rule. Moreover, he should give an example of humility to all.

[6] And if perhaps there is an issue about an appointment or some other matter in the monastery, [7] let him keep the place that he had when he entered the monastery and not that which was granted to him out of reverence for the priesthood.

[8] Also, if any clerics with the same desire want to join the monastery, they may be given a place in the middle, [9] but only if they themselves promise observance of the Rule and their own stability.

61. The Reception of Traveling Monks

If there arrives some traveling monk from provinces far away, and if he wants to live in the monastery as a guest, [2] and if he is content with the local customs which he finds, and does not, as can happen, disturb the monastery with his excessive demands, [3] but is simply content with what he finds, let him be received for as long as he desires.

[4] If, with sound reason and the humility of love, he sensibly offers some criticism or points out anything, let the abbot weigh the matter prudently, lest perhaps the Lord has sent him for this very thing.

[5] Later on, should he truly wish to establish his stability there, let such a wish not be denied, especially since it was possible to have some insight into his life during the time that he was a guest.

[6] But if he is found demanding and is full of evil ways during his time as a guest, he definitely must not be allowed to join the monastic community, [7] and moreover, he should also be told frankly that he should leave lest others be corrupted by his problems.

[8] If he is not one of those who deserves to be thrown out, he should, if he asks, not only be received as a member of the community, [9] but he should even be persuaded to stay so that others may be formed by his example, [10] for in every place we serve the one Lord and fight for the one King. [11] If the abbot also recognizes that he is deserving, he has the right to give him a place somewhat higher in seniority. [12] The abbot can give a place higher than that of their entrance not only to this monk, but also to those from the ranks of priests and clerics, noted above, if he perceives that their life deserves it.

[13] However, the abbot should take care that he never receives into his community a monk from another monastery known to him

without the consent of the monk's abbot or without letters of recommendation, [14] for it is written:

> What you do not want done to you, do not do to another. (Tob 4:16)

62. The Priests of the Monastery

If an abbot asks to have a priest or deacon ordained for himself, let him choose from his monks one who is worthy to carry out the priestly office.

[2] Let the one ordained beware of arrogance and pride, [3] and let him presume to do nothing unless the abbot has instructed him to do it, knowing that he will have to subject himself all the more to the discipline of the Rule. [4] Moreover, he should not let the priesthood become a reason to forget the obedience and discipline of the Rule; rather he should advance more and more toward God.

[5] Indeed, he should always keep the place that he had when he entered the monastery, [6] except for his service at the altar, and if perhaps the community chooses, or the abbot wants to move him up out of consideration for the merit of his life. [7] Nevertheless, he should know how to keep the rule set down for the deans and the prior. [8] Should he presume otherwise, let him be judged not as a priest but as a rebel.

[9] If he has been counseled often but does not set things right, let the bishop also be brought in as a witness. [10] If, after his faults have been repeatedly made clear to him and he still does not change, let him be cast out of the monastery—[11] but only if he has become so stubborn that he is unwilling to submit to or to obey the Rule.

63. Seniority in the Community

Let them keep their seniority in the monastery from the time of their *conversatio*, or according to the merit of their life, or as the abbot decides. [2] The abbot should not stir up the flock committed to him, nor should he unjustly put anything in place by the arbitrary use of power. [3] Rather, let him always bear in mind that he will have to render an account to God for all his decisions and deeds.

[4] Therefore, according to the seniority which the abbot has established or which they have, let the brothers approach for the sign of peace, for Communion, or to intone a psalm, or to stand in the choir. [5] In everything and everywhere, let age not determine or prejudice seniority, [6] for, as boys, Samuel and Daniel judged their elders (1 Sam 3; Dan 13:44-62).

[7] Therefore, except for those, as we have said, whom the abbot has promoted for higher motives or has demoted for certain reasons, all the rest should be in the order in which they began their *conversatio*. [8] As a result, for example, the one who came at the second hour of the day should realize that he is junior in the monastery to the one who came at the first hour of the day, whatever his age or dignity.

[9] The order for children should be maintained by everyone in everything.

[10] Therefore, let the juniors honor their seniors, and let the seniors love their juniors. [11] When calling each other by name, no one should be allowed to use just the name, [12] but seniors should call their juniors "brothers," and the juniors should call their seniors "*nonnus*" which means "reverend father."

[13] The abbot, however, since he is believed to act in the place of Christ, should be called lord and abbot, not because he has claimed it for himself, but for the honor and love of Christ. [14] He himself,

then, should reflect on this and present himself in such a way that he is worthy of such an honor.

[15] Whenever the brothers meet each other, the junior should ask a blessing of the senior. [16] When a senior passes by, the junior should rise and give him a place to sit; the junior should not presume to sit down unless his senior first bids him, [17] so that it may be as is written:

> Let them strive to be the first to show each other honor. (Rom 12:10)

[18] Small children and youths should follow their own seniority keeping good order in the oratory and at table. [19] Also, outside and everywhere, they are to be kept safe and in good order until they come to the age of understanding.

64. The Appointment of the Abbot

At the appointment of an abbot, always observe this principle: The person made abbot should be either the one elected according to the fear of God by the whole community with one heart, or elected by some part of the community with sounder judgment, however small. [2] Now the one appointed should be chosen for the merit of his life and for his teaching and wisdom, even though he may be last in the seniority of the community.

[3] If, God forbid, the whole community should conspire together and elect a person agreeing to their evil ways, [4] and if these evil ways should somehow come to the attention of the bishop to whose diocese the place belongs or to the abbots or Christians in the neighborhood, [5] let them take measures to prevent the plans of these wicked men from prevailing, and appoint a worthy steward over the house of God. [6] Let them know that they will receive a good reward if they do this with integrity and with godly zeal; on the other hand, they will sin if they do not deal with this.

[7] Once appointed, let the abbot always bear in mind what kind of burden he has accepted, and to whom he will have to *"render an account of his stewardship" (Luke 16:2)*; [8] and he should know that it is more important for him to be for others than to be over them.

[9] He must, therefore, be learned in the Divine Law so that he knows how to *"bring forth things new and old" (Matt 13:52)*. He is to be chaste, temperate, and merciful, [10] and he should always *"exalt mercy over judgment" (Jas 2:13)* so that he himself may find mercy.

[11] Let him hate their evil ways and love the brothers. [12] Now, when making a correction, let him act prudently and not go to excess, lest in his excessive desire to scrape off the rust he breaks the pot. [13] Let him always keep his own fragility before his eyes, and let him remember that *"the bruised reed must not be broken" (Isa 42:3)*. [14] By

this, we are not saying that he should permit evil ways to grow up, but he should cut them off with prudence and love as he sees best for each person, just as we have already said.

¹⁵ Also, let him strive to be loved rather than feared.

¹⁶ He must not be stormy or anxious, not extreme, or headstrong, not jealous or ever suspicious; otherwise he will never have rest. ¹⁷ In his commands, whether they concern God or the world, he should have foresight and consideration, and he should be discerning and moderate in the work he assigns, ¹⁸ bearing in mind the discretion of Holy Jacob when he said:

> If I drive my flocks too hard, they will all die in one day. (Gen 33:13)

¹⁹ Therefore, drawing on this and other witnesses to discretion, the mother of the virtues, let him so temper all things that both the strong have something to desire and the weak need not run away.

²⁰ And above all, let him keep this present Rule in all things, ²¹ so that when he has served well, he may hear from the Lord what the good servant heard who gave his fellow servants their bread at the proper time. ²² As he said:

> Amen, I say to you, he will set him over all his goods. (Matt 24:47)

65. The Prior of the Monastery

All too often, it happens that grave scandals arise in monasteries with the appointment of a prior, [2] for some, puffed up with the evil spirit of pride and considering themselves to be second abbots, assume absolute power for themselves, nourish scandals, and cause conflicts in the community.

[3] This happens especially in those places where the prior is also appointed by the same bishop or the same abbots who appointed the abbot. [4] The absurdity of this is easily grasped, because from the very outset of his appointment, he is given grounds for being proud, [5] in that his own thoughts insinuate to him that he is exempt from his abbot's authority: [6] "You too were appointed by those who also appointed the abbot."

[7] As a consequence, there arise envy, quarrels, slander, jealousy, conflicts, and disorder. [8] As a result, since the abbot and prior find themselves in opposition to each other, it necessarily follows that this conflict between them puts their souls in danger, [9] and those under them—while trying to please one or the other—go to their ruin. [10] The evil of these dangers rests first of all with those who made themselves the source of such confusion.

[11] Therefore, to safeguard peace and love, we see it as expedient that an appointment in his monastery should hinge on the abbot's decision. [12] And, if it can be done, as we have already arranged, let all the affairs of the monastery be managed by deans, just as the abbot arranges. [13] When this is entrusted to many, it follows that no one becomes proud.

[14] If, however, the place requires it, or the community asks with reason and humility, and the abbot judges it best, [15] then let the abbot himself, with the counsel of God-fearing brothers, appoint as his prior whomever he chooses. [16] Then let the prior carry out

with reverence those things that the abbot assigns him, while doing nothing contrary to the will or the appointment of the abbot, [17] for the more he is raised above the others, so much more must he be careful to keep the teachings of the Rule.

[18] If the prior is found full of evil ways, or, deceived by pride, if he becomes arrogant, or shows himself contemptuous of the Holy Rule, let him be counseled up to four times. [19] If he does not change, let the correction of the discipline of the Rule come to bear on him. [20] If even then he does not set things just right, let him be cast out of the office of prior, and let another who is worthy be called to take his place.

[21] If, after that, he is not peaceful and obedient in the community, let him even be expelled from the monastery. [22] Even so, the abbot should bear in mind that he is to render an account to God for all his decisions, lest perhaps the fire of envy or jealousy is burning in his soul.

66. The Porter of the Monastery

At the gate of the monastery, let there be stationed a wise old man who knows how to give and receive a message—someone whose advanced age keeps him from wandering about.

[2] This porter should have a cell next to the gate so that those coming may always find someone from whom they can get an answer. [3] As soon as anyone knocks or a poor person cries out, let him respond "Thanks be to God!" or "Bless me!" [4] And with all the gentleness of the fear of God, let him quickly respond with the warmth of love.

[5] If the porter has need, let him have a younger brother to help.

[6] Now a monastery, if it is possible, ought to be set up in such a way that it has everything necessary; that is, within the monastery there should be water, a mill, a garden; also various crafts should be pursued within the monastery. [7] As a result, the monks will have no need to wander outside because this is not at all good for their souls.

[8] Finally, we want this Rule read often in the community so that none of the brothers may make the excuse of ignorance.

67. Brothers Sent on a Journey

Brothers about to be sent on a journey should commend themselves to the prayer of all the brothers and the abbot. [2] Also, a remembrance of all those absent should always be made at the final prayer of the Work of God.

[3] On returning from a journey, the brothers on that same day are to lie on the floor of the oratory at the end of the Work of God for each of the canonical hours, [4] and they should ask the prayer of all for their transgressions, lest perhaps on the journey they found occasion to see something evil or to hear some idle talk.

[5] No one should presume to report to another what he may have seen or heard outside the monastery because it brings much destruction. [6] Should anyone presume to do this, let him be subject to the punishment of the Rule. [7] It should also be the same for anyone who presumes to leave the enclosure of the monastery or to go anywhere or to do anything, however small, without the abbot's command.

68. If Things Impossible Are Assigned to a Brother

If things, perhaps difficult or impossible, are assigned to a brother, he should certainly accept the command from the one making it with all gentleness and obedience. [2] But if he sees that the weight of the burden far exceeds the measure of his own strength, let him—with patience and at an opportune time—present to the one over him the reasons why he cannot possibly do it. [3] He should not become proud or unyielding or defiant.

[4] If, however, after he has made his case, the superior still thinks that there is reason for the command, let the junior know that this will be for his benefit, [5] and confident in the help of God, let him obey out of love.

69. No One is to Presume to Defend Another

Let every precaution be taken so that no one in the monastery presumes, under any circumstance, to defend another monk or become, as it were, his protector, [2] even though they are closely connected by blood.

[3] Let the monks not presume to do this in any way whatsoever because it can give rise to the most grievous scandals. [4] Should anyone cross this line, let him be kept strictly under control.

70. No One is to Presume to Strike Another Arbitrarily

Let every opportunity for presumption be shunned, [2] and we decree that no one is permitted to excommunicate or to strike any of his brothers unless the abbot has given him the authority. [3] Moreover, *"sinners are to be called out before all so that the others may have fear"* (1 Tim 5:20).

[4] By all means, everyone should keep safe the young up to the age of fifteen, and take care for their good order; [5] yet this, too, should be done with all measure and good sense. [6] If someone older, without the abbot's direction and without discretion, flares up against the young, let him be subject to the discipline of the Rule, [7] because it is written,

> *What you do not want done to yourself, do not do to another.* (Tob 4:16)

71. That the Brothers Be Obedient to One Another

The good of obedience should be shown by all, not just to the abbot, but the brothers should also obey each other in the same way, [2] knowing that by this way of obedience they will go to God.

[3] We do not permit private commands to supersede a command already given by the abbot or the superiors whom he has assigned. [4] In other situations, let all the juniors obey their seniors with all love and concern. [5] If anyone is found contentious, let him be corrected.

[6] Now if any brother is corrected in any way by the abbot or by any other senior for any reason, however small, [7] or if he even senses that any senior is angered or disturbed by him, however little, [8] let him immediately and without delay cast himself on the ground at his feet and continue to lie there making satisfaction until this disturbance is healed by a blessing.

[9] But if anyone scorns doing this, either he should be subjected to corporal punishment, or, if he is stubborn, he should be expelled from the monastery.

72. The Good Zeal That Monks Must Have

1 Just as there is an evil zeal of bitterness which separates from God and leads to hell, [2] so there is a good zeal which separates from evil ways and leads to God and everlasting life.

[3] Let monks, therefore, practice this zeal with the warmest love.

[4] That is, let them *"strive to be the first to show each other honor"* (*Rom 12:10*).

[5] Let them bear most patiently with one another's weaknesses, whether of body or of character.

[6] Let them devote themselves to the rivalry of obedience to one another.

[7] No one should follow what he judges useful for himself, but what is better for the other.

[8] Let them devote themselves to the chaste love of the brothers.

[9] In love let them fear God.

[10] Let them love their abbot with a sincere and humble love.

[11] Let them prefer nothing whatever to Christ, [12] and may he bring us all alike to everlasting life.

73. The Observance of All Justice Is Not Set Down in This Rule

We have written down this Rule so that by keeping it in monasteries, we may show that, to some degree, we possess an integrity of character and the beginning of *conversatio*.

[2] As for those who are hurrying toward the perfection of *conversatio*, there are the teachings of the fathers whose observance may lead a person to the heights of perfection. [3] For what page or what word of divine authority in the Old or New Testament is not the most perfect standard of human life? [4] Or what book of the holy, catholic fathers does not resound with this, so that we may, by this straight path, reach our Creator? [5] Are there not the *Conferences* of the Fathers and their *Institutes* and *Lives* as well as the Rule of our Holy Father Basil? [6] What else are they than the tools of the virtues for monks who obey and live good lives?

[7] But for us, the lazy and careless who live badly, there is the blush of shame.

[8] Therefore, whoever you may be, as you rush to the heavenly homeland, carry out with the help of Christ this smallest Rule written down for beginners.

[9] Then, at length, as we have pointed out above, you will, with God as your protector, arrive at the loftier summits of teaching and virtues. Amen.

Chapter 58 has the novice master read the Rule to the novices three times during the year of their probation. Many monastic communities and others follow this practice and read the Rule three times during the course of the year according to the schema given below. If you click on the reading for a given day, it will link you to the reading.

P.1-7: Jan. 1, May 2, Sept. 1

P.8-13: Jan. 2, May 3, Sept. 2

P.14-20: Jan. 3, May 4, Sept. 3

P.21-32: Jan. 4, May 5, Sept. 4

P.33-38: Jan. 5, May 6, Sept. 5

P.39-44: Jan. 6, May 7, Sept. 6

P.45-50: Jan. 7, May 8, Sept. 7

1.1-12: Jan. 8, May 9, Sept. 8

2.1-6: Jan. 9, May 10, Sept. 9

2.7-10: Jan. 10, May 11, Sept. 10

2.11-15: Jan. 11, May 12, Sept. 11

2.16-22: Jan. 12, May 13, Sept. 12

2.23-29: Jan. 13, May 14, Sept. 13

2.30-32: Jan. 14, May 15, Sept. 14

2.33-40: Jan. 15, May 16, Sept. 15

3.1-6 — Jan. 16, May 17, Sept. 16

3.7-13 — Jan. 17, May 18, Sept. 17

4.1-21 — Jan. 18, May 19, Sept. 18

4.22-43 — Jan. 19, May 20, Sept. 19

4.44-61 — Jan. 20, May 21, Sept. 20

4.62-78 — Jan. 21, May 22, Sept. 21

5.1-13 — Jan. 22, May 23, Sept. 22

5.14-19 — Jan. 23, May 24, Sept. 23

6.1-8 — Jan. 24, May 25, Sept. 24

7.1-9 — Jan. 25, May 26, Sept. 25

7.10-11 — Jan. 26, May 27, Sept. 26

7.12-18 — Jan. 27, May 28, Sept. 27

7.19-23 — Jan. 28, May, 29, Sept. 28

7.24-30 — Jan. 29, May 30, Sept. 29

7.31-33 — Jan. 30, May 31, Sept. 30

7.34 — Jan. 31, June 1, Oct. 1

7.35-43 — Feb. 1, June 2, Oct. 2

7.44-48 — Feb. 2, June 3, Oct. 3

7.49-50 — Feb. 3, June 4, Oct. 4

7.51-54 — Feb. 4, June 5, Oct. 5

7.55 — Feb. 5, June 6, Oct. 6

7.56-58 — Feb. 6, June 7, Oct. 7

7.59 — Feb. 7, June 8, Oct. 8

7.60-61 — Feb. 8, June 9, Oct. 9

7.62-70 — Feb. 9, June 10, Oct. 10

8.1-4 — Feb. 10, June 11, Oct. 11

9.1-11 — Feb. 11, June 12, Oct. 12

10.1-3 — Feb. 12, June 13, Oct. 13

11.1-13 — Feb. 13, June 14, Oct. 14

12.1-3 — Feb. 14, June 15, Oct. 15

13:1-11 — Feb. 15, June 16, Oct. 16

13:12-14 — Feb. 16, June 17, Oct. 17

14:1-2 — Feb. 17, June 18, Oct. 18

15:1-4 — Feb. 18, June 19, Oct. 19

16.1-5 — Feb. 19, June 20, Oct. 20

17.1-10 — Feb. 20, June 21, Oct. 21

18.1-6 — Feb. 21, June 22, Oct. 22

18.7-11 — Feb. 22, June 23, Oct. 23

18.12-19 — Feb. 23, June 24, Oct. 24

18.20-25 — Feb. 24 in leap year, June 25, Oct. 25

19.1-7 — Feb. 24 (leap year 25), June 26, Oct. 26

20:1-5 — Feb. 25 (leap year 26), June 27, Oct. 27

21.1-7 — Feb. 26 (leap year 27), June 28, Oct. 28

22.1-8 — Feb. 27 (leap year 28), June 29, Oct. 29

23.1-5 — Feb. 28 (leap year 29), June 30, Oct. 30

24.1-7 — Mar. 1, July 1, Oct. 31

25.1-6 — Mar. 2, July 2, Nov. 1

26.1-2 — Mar. 3, July 3, Nov. 2

27.1-9 — Mar. 4, July 4, Nov. 3

28.1-8 — Mar. 5, July 5, Nov. 4

29.1-3 — Mar. 6, July 6, Nov. 5

30.1-3 — Mar. 7, July 7, Nov. 6

31.1-12 — Mar. 8, July 8, Nov. 7

31.13-19 —Mar. 9, July 9, Nov. 8

32.1-5 — Mar. 10, July 10, Nov. 9

33.1 — Mar. 11, July 11, Nov. 10

34.1-7 — Mar. 12, July 12, Nov. 11

35.1-11 — Mar. 13, July 13, Nov. 12

35.12-18 — Mar. 14, July 14, Nov. 13

36.1-10 — Mar. 15, July 15, Nov. 14

37.1-2 — Mar. 16, July 16, Nov. 15

38.1-12 — Mar. 17, July 17, Nov. 16

39.1-11 — Mar. 18, July 18, Nov. 17

40.1-9 — Mar. 19, July 19, Nov. 18

41.1-9 — Mar. 20, July 20, Nov. 19

42.1-11 — Mar. 21, July 21, Nov. 20

43.1-12 — Mar. 22, July 22, Nov. 21

43.13-19 — Mar. 23, July 23, Nov. 22

44.1-10 — Mar. 24, July 24, Nov. 23

45.1-3 — Mar. 25, July 25, Nov. 24

46.1-6 — Mar. 26, July 26, Nov. 25

47.1-4 — Mar. 27, July 27, Nov. 26

48.1-9 — Mar. 28, July 28, Nov. 27

48.10-21 — Mar. 29, July 29, Nov. 28

48.22-25 — Mar. 30, July 30, Nov. 29

49.1-10 — Mar. 31, July 31, Nov. 30

50.1-4 — Apr. 1, Aug. 1, Dec. 1

51.1-3 — Apr. 2, Aug. 2, Dec. 2

52.1-5 — Apr. 3, Aug. 3, Dec. 3

53.1-15 — Apr. 4, Aug. 4, Dec. 4

53.16-24 — Apr. 5, Aug. 5, Dec. 5

54.1-5 — Apr. 6, Aug. 6, Dec. 6

55.1-14 — Apr. 7, Aug. 7, Dec. 7

55:15-22 — Apr. 8, Aug. 8, Dec. 8

56.1-3 — Apr. 9, Aug. 9, Dec. 9

57.1-9 — Apr. 10, Aug. 10, Dec. 10

58.1-16 — Apr. 11, Aug. 11, Dec. 11

58.17-29 — Apr. 12, Aug. 12, Dec. 12

59.1-8 — Apr. 13, Aug. 13, Dec. 13

60.1-9 — Apr. 14, Aug. 14, Dec. 14

61.1-5 — Apr. 15, Aug. 15, Dec. 15

61.6-14 — Apr. 16, Aug. 16, Dec. 16

62.1-11 — Apr. 17, Aug. 17, Dec. 17

63.1-9 — Apr. 18, Aug. 18, Dec. 18

63.10-19 — Apr. 19, Aug. 19, Dec. 19

64.1-6 — Apr. 20, Aug. 20, Dec. 20

64.7-22 — Apr. 21, Aug. 21, Dec. 21

65.1-10 — Apr. 22, Aug. 22, Dec. 22

65.11-22 — Apr. 23, Aug. 23, Dec. 23

66.1-8 — Apr. 24, Aug. 24, Dec. 24

67.1-7 — Apr. 25, Aug. 25, Dec. 25

68.1-5 — Apr. 26, Aug. 26, Dec. 26

69.1-4 — Apr. 27, Aug. 27, Dec. 27

70.1-7 — Apr. 28, Aug. 28, Dec. 28

71.1-9 — Apr. 29, Aug. 29, Dec. 29

72.1-12 — Apr. 30, Aug. 30, Dec. 30

73.1-9 — May 1, Aug. 31, Dec. 31

Colophon

Fr. Hilary de Jean, OSB, made the original Saint Meinrad translation and published it in 1937. He later transferred his stability to Saint Joseph Abbey in St. Benedict, LA.

In 1956, Grail Publications at Saint Meinrad printed the translation with a note that it had been revised in 1950. That revision mainly included an updating of the Scripture references from the translation of the Confraternity of Christian Doctrine.

This revision follows Fr. Hilary's goal of remaining close to the Latin as addressed to the original audience and context. Translations of the mid- and late-20th century have sought a more idiomatic translation, while more recent versions have adopted an inclusive approach which has precedents in the tradition. Each approach has its advantages.

The *Rule* follows the numbering of the psalms in the Septuagint and Vulgate. They have been adjusted to follow the numbering in the Hebrew, as found in translations today.

Fr. Harry Hagan, OSB, made this revision. Various monks reviewed the first draft and offered many helpful comments that greatly improved the revision: Fr. Vincent Tobin, OSB, Fr. Colman Grabert, OSB, Fr. Guerric DeBona, OSB, Fr. Eugene Hensell, OSB, Br. Francis de Sales Wagner, OSB, and Fr. Mateo Zamora, OSB. The text was also reviewed by Fr. Aelred Kavanagh, OSB, of Saint Joseph Abbey, and Fr. Joel Rippinger, OSB, of Marmion Abbey.

Br. Francis de Sales Wagner, OSB, also served as the copy editor and a proofreader. Fr. Mateo Zamora, OSB, and Mrs. Mary Jeanne Schumacher also assisted as proofreaders.

This revision follows the Latin text given in the RB 1980 taken from the Latin text of Jean Neufville in *La Règle de Saint Benoît*, Sources Chrétiennes, 181-182. Paris: Les Éditions du Cerf, 1972.

The following translations especially were consulted:

Fry, Timothy, ed. *RB 1980: The Rule of St. Benedict in Latin and English with Notes.* Collegeville, MN: The Liturgical Press, 1981.

Holzherr, Georg. *Die Benediktsregel. Eine Anleitung zu christlichem Leben.* Freiburg, Switzerland: Paulusverlag, 1982. English: *The Rule of Benedict: An Invitation to the Christian Life,* translated by Mark Thamert. Cistercian Studies, 256. Collegeville, MN: Cistercian Publications/Liturgical Press, 2016.

Kardong, Terrence G., tr. *Benedict's Rule: A Translation and Commentary.* Collegeville, MN: The Liturgical Press, 1996.

Lentini, Anselm, tr. & ed. *La Regola.* Montecassino: Publicazaioni Cassinesi, 1994.

Probst, Benedikt, ed. *Regula Benedicti de codice 914 in bibliotheca monasterii S. Galli.* St. Ottilien: EOS Verlag, 1982.

Puzicha, Michaela, Joannes Gartner, Plazidus Hungerbühler, tr. and ed. *Quellen und Texte zur Benediktusregel.* St. Ottilien: EOS Verlag, 2007.

Venarde, Bruce L., ed. and tr. *The Rule of Saint Benedict.* Dumbarton Oaks Medieval Library, 6. Cambridge, MA: Harvard University Press, 2011.

Vogüé, Adalbert de, tr. *La Règle de Saint Benoît.* Sources Chrétiennes, 181 and 182. Paris: Les Éditions du Cerf, 1972.

Biography of Harry Hagan, OSB

Fr. Harry Hagan, OSB, SSD, is a monk and priest of Saint Meinrad Archabbey. He is an associate professor of Scripture at Saint Meinrad Seminary and School of Theology. He holds a Doctorate in Sacred Scripture from the Pontifical Biblical Institute in Rome. Additionally, he received a Master of Divinity from Saint Meinrad Seminary and a Master of Arts in Religious Studies from Indiana University. His undergraduate work was in English at Saint Meinrad College.

While teaching, he has also served as dean of students and vice rector in the seminary and as novice and junior master in the monastery. In addition to articles in the areas of Scripture and monastic studies, he has published more than forty texts for hymns.

Fr. Harry can be reached at hhagan@saintmeinrad.edu.

Made in the USA
Columbia, SC
14 April 2025

56646121R00080